THE PROGRESSIVE
EDUCATION MOVEMENT

GARLAND REFERENCE LIBRARY
OF SOCIAL SCIENCE
(VOL. 29)

THE PROGRESSIVE EDUCATION MOVEMENT
An Annotated Bibliography

Mariann Pezzella Winick

GARLAND PUBLISHING, INC. · NEW YORK & LONDON
1978

Library of Congress Cataloging in Publication Data

Winick, Mariann P
  The progressive education movement.

  (Garland reference library of social science; v. 29)
  Includes index.
  1. Education—Philosophy—Bibliography. I. Title.
Z5811.W55 [LB7]   016.3701   76-24764
ISBN 0-8240-9913-3

Printed in the United States of America

This book is dedicated to Dr. Robert F. Petluck, educator extraordinaire, Dora Rodetsky and Dorothy Abramson, who led their students to believe that learning was the ultimate adventure, and to my classmates at P. S. 8, The Bronx, New York City (1935–1942), remembered friends in a grand experience in living and learning:

Louise Fink	Robert Albrecht
Janet Lee	Harry Cahill
Joan Meyers	Frederick Caplan
Camille Monaco	Peter Caruso
Lillian Preinsberger	Anthony Charimella
Carmella Santora	Jerry DeCaprio
Jane Shaw	Joel Greenberg
Marion Sommers	Ernest Helmreich
Ellen Sonnick	Irving Heps
Marilyn Steinman	Stanley Kaufman
Joan Weiss	Louis Kislak
Iris Werner	Robert Loehman
Mildred Zambardino	David Schultz
	Eugene Sloan
	William Staudinger

CONTENTS

PREFACE

The Progressive Education Movement appears as one of those truly American artifacts, the patchwork quilt: bits and pieces of older garments (some from the old country) and snips of new cloth, interestingly positioned shapes and color forming a whole, providing substance and service for the present and future. In a sense, there is no precise beginning to the Progressive Education Movement, since its antecedents come from sources so varied in time, place and intent. There is, however, a need to set parameters for the purposes of a bibliography. The last several decades of the nineteenth century reflect the thrust of scientists to position man in terms of his development. Similarly, among educators and social scientists, the possibility of relating stages of the development of mankind to a growing focus on the individual set the stage for a scientific approach to education. This approach surfaced almost simultaneously in England, America, Italy, Germany, France and Belgium. The beginning of the twentieth century emerges as a decisive point in the coalescing of ideas.

In Sweden, Ellen Kay wrote a serious volume, *The Century of the Child* (1901), which set the catchword for the century. Meeting the individual's needs is one of the basic thrusts of the early progressives. In America, the focus on child study marshalled by G. Stanley Hall at Clark University set a phalanx of students and faculty in search of a better understanding of the child. Francis Parker, sometimes called the Father of Progressive Education, undertook the reformation of the Quincy, Massachusetts, schools in 1875 along newer, more progressive lines. John Dewey (1896), moving from a different direction, wanted to examine education in terms of an analysis of thought process and devise approaches to integrate learning through the school experience. Reddie, in England (1898), looked to goals beyond the academic in shaping Abbotsholme, which was to become an experimental learning community. In 1905 the schools in Mannheim, Germany, were organized on child study lines, allowing classes to be formed on the basis of children's individual abilities. Claparede, in Geneva (1903), devoted himself to experimental pedagogy and attempted to influence those currently teaching through newer child-centered approaches. In France, M. Binet, Director of Primary Education, set up experimental situations and devised means of measurement to evaluate such educational innovations. Montessori, in Italy, having developed her ideas through an early interest in anthropology, began an experiment in individualized instruction and reevaluation of the classroom teacher's role that was to provide material for development for the remainder of the century (1907). In Spain, an ultimately martyred Francesco Ferrar founded a journal, *L'Ecole Renovée*, which was published in Paris in 1908.

The needs of industrialists to provide for the assimilation of an immigrant and unskilled population into the labor force gave William Wirt an opportunity to develop the Work-Study-Play synthesis that became known as the "Gary Plan" (1908). Labor was an important consideration in educational planning, and Marietta Johnson in 1907 assessed the needs of a rural population and developed changes that had broad ramifications for the trends which followed in rural administration and planning.

By 1919 a formalized group known as the Progressive Education Association came into being. Its power was to last for a quarter of a century as a national force in educational decision making. Similarly, in England, Beatrice Ensor initiated the New Education Fellowship, an international organization devoted to progressive changes. The publications of both of these groups, as well as their conferences and committees, help to provide for dissemination of research and activities throughout the world.

The impact of rapidly changing social needs became an important force in the Progressive Education Movement. With the end of World War I and the major worldwide shifts in economic and political leadership, the educational system of a country was seen as a highly "usable" tool in reformulations of national goals.

In America, the growing differences between those interested in the growth of the individual and those interested in the needs of a society made for a major division in the cohesiveness of the Progressive Education Association.

One of the more startling findings while working on this compilation was the realization that the changed social order in Germany (Nazism) was seen by some influential American educators as a positive reflection of the way in which progressive educational ideas could help serve national goals (Germany, Russia, even China, at a later period, were reported on with enthusiasm).

Dewey himself became critical of the apparent neglect of the scientific aspects of systematic study by the thirties. During the late thirties, experiments flourished. Some were recorded, others forgotten, and still others criticized. A growing sense of diffuse educational goals was reflected in the critical and/or defensive quality of the writing of this time. The Depression was experienced in a variety of ways. The focus on social justice and equality loomed as a larger task for the schools than the reform of teaching techniques. Despite the fact that individual schools and school systems sustained their progressive efforts and purposes, the educators of the nation appeared to have forgotten early successes and moved in wider and wider spheres away from a science of education.

Individual countries in Europe had experienced the traumatic effects of World War II, and the problems of reconstruction did not favor the experimental approach. The prominence of education as a major force in the development of power in Nazi Germany helped to downgrade the use of educational systems as part of socio-political development. Most countries reverted to formal school curricula and techniques. Not until the fifties did Great Britain become the focus for the first reemergence of the progressive spirit as seen in the open-classroom movement.

This bibliography was undertaken to help provide a sense of the aspects of the movement that have often been obscured by the theoretical and philosophical investigations. Little has been

written assessing the curricula, administrative practices and
evaluation techniques developed by such an internationally important educational movement. The bibliography is divided into
sections to help the reader deal with particular aspects of the
movement. Crosslistings are indicated since the material is often
useful in a variety of ways. The entries appear as sequentially
numbered and are referred to in the author index by number
rather than page. The areas covered are; History, Philosophy,
Theory, Comparative, Criticism, Curriculum, Teacher Training,
Evaluation and Record-keeping, Experimental Schools, Administration, Parent Involvement, Journals.

As a former student in one of the many experimental situations, my sense of objectivity is somewhat skewed. Full responsibility for the selections and omissions (the hidden terror of a
bibliographer), however, is mine. I have attempted to fit the
pieces and form a serviceable work. It would have been a lonely
task were it not for the support and kind attentions of my col-
league, Dr. Abigail S. Woods. Valuable aid and advice were
welcomed from Dr. William Myrick and Ms. Bertha Bendelstein
of the Brooklyn College Library. The Elmer Bobst Library of
New York University was made available to me as a visiting
scholar; its resources in this area were most welcome. To Laura
and Raphael Winick special appreciation should be stated for
both their help and tolerance.

THE PROGRESSIVE
EDUCATION MOVEMENT

A HISTORY

1   Adams, Harold J. "The Progressive Heritage of Guid-
     ance: A View from the Left", *Personnel and Guid-
     ance Journal*, Vol. 51, No. 8, April, 1973, 531-
     538.

     A comparison and evaluation of the ideals of the
     progressives and those of the counseling movement:
     an emphasis on access to opportunity and pluralism,
     pragmatism, adjustment and on the individual. These
     dimensions are examined in terms of larger social
     goals. An interesting review article.

2   Alberty, Harold B. *A Study of the Project Method
     in Education*. Columbus: The Ohio State Univer-
     sity Press, 1927, 111 pp.

     An attempt to place the project method into per-
     spective through an examination and evaluation of
     the method from an historical viewpoint. The rela-
     tionship of real life learning to text learning is
     presented. A substantive contribution which includes
     a review of selected research. The relationship of
     methodology to development of thought processes is a
     strongly developed area.

3   Anderson, John E. "Child Development: An Historical
     Perspective", *Child Development*, Vol. XXVII, No.
     2, 1956, 181-196.

     The beginnings of the child-centered educational
     movement are traced through an examination of the
     child development literature of the nineteenth cen-
     tury.

4   Anonymous. *Sanderson of Oundle*. New York: The
     Macmillan Company, 1923, 365 pp.

     A descriptive volume of the work and personality
     of F. W. Sanderson, Headmaster of Oundle, by anony-
     mous students and admirers. The work of Sanderson
     in opening the doors of Oundle to change through a new

philosophy is sympathetically described. The final
chapter, a speech given by Sanderson, provides primary material on his ideas, ideals and vision. Work
as a higher force, creativity, individual responsibility are strongly supported in his educational
plan. As a prominent educator of the New Era, Sanderson looms as an intriguing figure.

5   Bagley, William. *Education, Crime, and Social Pro-
        gress.* New York: The Macmillan Company, 1931,
        150 pp.

     An interesting volume addressing the issue of
"discipline" within the framework of society and
schools. The writer presents his data and ideas related to respect for law internationally and nation-
ally. Treatment of progressive educational ideals
from an historical framework is provided. An interesting appendix deals with crime statistics.

6   Bowden, A. O. et al. *Bibliographies on Educational
        Sociology.* Buffalo: State Teachers College,
        1928, 154 pp.

     This first yearbook of the National Society for
the Study of Educational Sociology was designed to
help define the area. It provides complementary
readings for those interested in progressive education since the educational determinants of the time
were so closely connected to sociological processes.
The bibliography begins in 1893 and includes both
journal and text citations. While some of the citations are haphazard, the material covered is vast:
under major institutions of education   work conducted through family life, museums, churches, foundations, libraries, adult education help to round out
the social movement in which progressive education
operated.

7   Bowers, C. A. *The Progressive Educator and the De-
        pression: The Radical Years.* New York: Random
        House, 1939, 269 pp.

     The effects of the social and economic climate on
teachers and the schools during the Depression. The
radicalization of the progressive movement is discussed.

8   Bowers, C. A. "Social Reconstructionism: Views from
        the Left and the Right, 1932-1942", *History of
        Education Quarterly,* Vol. 10, No. 1, Spring, 1970,
        22-52.

A far-ranging analysis of the progressive education movement in terms of the changes in social a-
wareness and the need to re-define the role of the
citizen in a democracy. An historical perspective
of the social change aspect of the movement.

9   Boyd, William and W. Rawson. *The Story of the New
     Education*. London: Heinemann, 1965, 202 pp.

     A re-accounting of the newer educational prac-
tices and ideas of the first part of the twentieth
century. The authors' attempt to create an in-depth
picture of change as reflected in the convergence of
different educational thinkers. A general historical development of the New Education Fellowship is
covered in detail.

10   Boydston, JoAnn. "Notes and Documents I: John Dewey
     and the Journals", *History of Education Quarterly*,
     Vol. 10, No. 1, Spring, 1970, 72-77.

     A rich resource listing and commenting on the dif-
ferent publications in which Dewey's 766 articles appeared. Annotations are on the publications, not on
individual articles.

11   Brameld, Theodore. *Ends and Means in Education*: A
     Midcentury Appraisal. New York: Harper and
     Brothers, 1950, 244 pp.

     A retrospective view, as well as a status of
education at midcentury. The thoughts of educators
involved in education as reconstruction emerge in a
free-wheeling appraisal of the past.

12   Brickman, William (ed.) *John Dewey: Master Educa-
     tor*. New York: Society for the Advancement of
     Education, 1959, 172 pp.

     A collection of essays, originally presented in
the SCHOOL AND SOCIETY, October 10, 1959, commera-
tive issue on Dewey's centennial. These eleven papers provide a composite picture of Dewey on education. Maxine Green's review of the 1894-1920 period
sets the period and the personalities into perspective.

13   Broudy, H. S. "Democratic Values and Educational
     Goals", *Curriculum: 70th Yearbook*. National
     Society for the Study of Education. Chicago:
     University of Chicago Press, 1971, 113-152.

     A clear, concise examination of the development
of democratic values through education. A re-examin-

ation of the work of Dewey and the progressives in terms of the fifties shift. The political and economic factors surrounding the attacks of the fifties experienced by the progressive movement are related to larger societal shifts. Stimulating, pertinent and provoking material.

14   Butts, R. Freeman and Lawrence A. Cremin. *A History of Education in American Culture*. New York: Holt and Company, 1953, 628 pp.

A basic text addressing itself to specific problems in American education in terms of its historical development. The twentieth century is well covered. This text was a popular basic resource in the fifties.

15   Cremin, Lawrence A. *The Transformation of the School: Progressivism in American Education, 1876-1957*. New York: Alfred A. Knopf, Inc., 1961, 387 pp.

A detailed accounting of the pluralistic nature of the progressive education movement in America. The shift in the role schools were to play in a fluid society is described through an examination of the historical, political and intellectual thinking of the late 1800's and the first half of the twentieth century. An excellent resource is to be found in the Bibliographical Notes.

16   DePancier, Ida. *The History of the Laboratory Schools, The University of Chicago, 1896-1965*. Chicago: Quadrangle Books, 1967, 207 pp.

A chronicle of the pioneering and germanitive work at the famed University of Chicago Laboratory School, originally the Dewey School. While this is a more recent book than the Mayhew text of the Dewey School, the earlier book covers greater area.

17   Dropkin, Ruth and Arthur Obier (eds.) *Roots of Open Education in America*. New York: Workshop Center for Open Education, City College of New York, 1976, 201 pp.

A collection of accounts on the antecedents of open education in America. Interviews with progressive educators of the twenties and thirties. Selected bibliography included.

18   Drost, Walter H. "A Visit with Stanwood Cobb", *Educational Forum*, Vol. 35, No. 3, March, 1971, 287-294.

An interview with Stanwood Cobb, past president of the Progressive Education Association in which he

discusses the innovative work at the Chevy Chase
Country Day School and the beginnings of progressive
education in the Capitol area.

19   Good, H. G. *A History of American Education.* New
      York: The Macmillan Company, 1962, 610 pp.

      An interesting textbook covering developments in
American education. Particular emphasis on the problems and issues of the twentieth century make this
volume useful in terms of better understanding of
the dynamics of the progressive era.

20   Goodenow, Ronald. "The Progressive Educator, Race
      and Ethnicity in the Depression Years: An Over-
      view", *History of Education Quarterly*, Vol. 15,
      No. 4, Winter, 1975, 365-394.

      An interesting assessment of the Progressive
Education Association and the progressive movement
in general in relation to attitudes of white educators during the thirties toward the schooling of
minority and ethnic groups. The role of the black
educator in the South with regard to progressive
changes in southern schools is discussed.

21   Graham, Patricia Albjerg. *Progressive Education:
      From Arcady to Academe.* New York: Teachers
      College Press, 1967, 193 pp.

      A detailed history of the Progressive Education
Association from 1919 to 1955. The functions of
the Association, its philosophical stand, its political and social leanings and commitments are examined in terms of the passage of time. A definitive
work on the Association. Appendices include listing
of commissions and committees of the Association. A
bibliographic essay includes material on published
and unpublished materials.

22   Greene, Maxine. "Dewey and American Education:
      1894-1920", *School and Society*, Vol. 87, 1959,
      381-386.

      A summary article on the effect of Dewey's ideas
and philosophy on educational practices.

23   Horowitz, Helen. "The Progressive Education Movement
      after World War I", *Times (London) Educational
      Supplement*, No. 2912, April 30, 1971, 78-84.

      Reviews of histories on the progressive education
movement.

24   Hulbard, David. *This Happened in Pasedena*. New
        York: The Macmillan Company, 1951, 166 pp.

        An accounting of the firing of William Goslin,
Superintendent of Schools in Pasedena in 1950. The
work of the progressives was used as a weapon against
this administrator.

25   Hymes, James L. Jr. and Frederick L. Redefer. "The
        Progressive Education Association", *Childhood
        Education*, Vol. 52, No. 1, October, 1955, 25-28.

        A lively interview of Redefer by Hymes. The his-
tory, philosophy and activities of the Association
are discussed. This development through the twenties
and thirties is carefully addressed. The demise of
the Association is detailed in an affectionate and
clear manner.

26   Kavier, Clarence J. "Elite View of American Educa-
        tion", *Journal of Contemporary History*, Vol. 2,
        July, 1967, 201-217.

        An unusual treatment, in retrospect, of the un-
folding of American education during the first quarter of the century. The paper deals with an historical perspective that adds to an understanding of the
progressive movement within its time.

27   LaBrant, Lou. "A Word of Protest", *Teachers College
        Record*, Vol. 74, No. 2, December, 1972, 167-169.

        In this short article the author requests that
educators would do well to return to the literature
of the 1920's and 1930's in order to bypass some of
the errors committed in the past and to profit from
the richly documented experiences of that period.

28   Lawson, M. D. and R. C. Peterson. *Progressive Educa-
        tion: An Introduction*. Sydney, Australia: Angus
        and Robertson, 1972.

        A lucid exploration of what progressive education
means, providing both an historical and current view
of theorists and classroom practices. The material
on Dewey is long overdue. Montessori is placed into
perspective and Helen Parkhurst's work is accurately
described. The contemporary quality of the DeCroly
"centers of interest" is surprising. The final chapter presents "a blueprint for a progressive school".
A progressive education timeline is provided as well
as a bibliography.

29   Lilge, Frederick. "John Dewey, 1859-1959: Reflec-
        tions on His Educational and Social Thought",

Educational Forum, XXIV, March, 1960, 351-356.

An examination of social trends and influences affecting and reflecting Dewey's ideas. Attitudes toward social reform and the relationship of education to such reform are described.

30   Lord Allen of Hurtwood (ed.) *Learning to Live Together*. London: New Education Fellowship, 1936, 136 pp.

An accounting of the Dutch New Education Conference at Utrecht in 1936. The problems involved in greater interpersonal and international skills are described. In terms of the historical (1936) significance of the meeting the material is of interest in adding some light to the ideas and plans of educators prior to World War II.

31   Meiklejohn, Alexander. *Education Between Two Worlds*. New York: Atherton Press, 1966 Edition, 303 pp.

An interesting comparative study of the educational theories of John Dewey and Jean Jacques Rousseau.

32   Meyer, Adolphe. *The Development of Education in the Twentieth Century*. New York: Prentice-Hall, Inc., 1940, 406 pp.

An accounting of modern education including material on Dewey, Mearns, Kilpatrick, Cizek and Dalcroze. The text on the Associated Experimental Schools (City and Country, Walden, Little Red Schoolhouse, Hessian Hills and the Harriet Johnson Nursery) is particularly enlightening. The work of the Bureau of Educational Experimentation is described. Some material on foreign schools in included.

33   Mitchell, Lucy Sprague. *Two Lives: The Story of Wesley Claire Mitchell and Myself*. New York: Simon & Schuster, 1953, 575 pp.

A biography and an autobiography that helps to illuminate the life and work of Lucy Sprague Mitchell, one of the founders of the Bank Street Schools. The years from 1913-1944 were very productive years and the author describes her work at the Bureau of Educational Experiments as Chairman and her close relationships with Caroline Pratt at the City and Country School, Elizabeth Irwin at the Little Red Schoolhouse, and as innovator of the Bank Street Workshops. A highly personal accounting providing insight into some of the relationships and inter-relationships among New York innovators during the Pre-World War II period.

34   Monroe, Paul. *A Cyclopedia of Education* (5 Volumes).
      New York: The Macmillan Company, 1911, 726 pp.
      Re-published, Gale Research Company, 1968.

      A five-volume resource of educational terminology,
      programs, personages. A rich, historical source for
      Pre-World War I information.

35   Monroe, Walter. *Bibliographies and Summaries of Edu-
      cation.* New York: H. W. Wilson & Company, 1936,
      470 pp.

      A basic resource listing important contributors in
      education and descriptive material on educational prac-
      tices and trends.

36   Pinck, Dan. "Plus Sa Change...", *Saturday Review of
      Literature,* Vol. 55, No. 42, November, 1972, 36.

      A short review of the educational changes in the
      Gary Schools circa 1916. The changes are paralleled
      with contemporary changes. The contrast is interest-
      ing.

37   Progressive Education Association. *Growth and Devel-
      opment: The Basis for Educational Programs.* New
      York: Progressive Education Association, 1936,
      292 pp.

      A collection of papers prepared for the Chicago
      Association for Child Study and Parent Education and
      the Progressive Education Conference of 1936. These
      forty-eight papers cover an enormous range of topics.
      The developmental needs of children are central to
      each article. Anecdotal situations are used frequently
      to illustrate specific points. The volume has an im-
      portant position in the literature of the time.

38   Reisner, Edward. "What is Progressive Education?",
      Teachers College Record, Vol. XXXV, 1933-1934,
      192-201.

      The relationship of the educational movement to that
      of progressivism in examined in terms of the early roots
      of such reform.

39   Reschly, Dan and Darrell Sabers. "Open Education:
      Have We Been There Before?", *Phi Delta Kappan,*
      Vol. 55, No. 10, June, 1974, 675-677.

      A detailed comparison of open education and progres-
      sive education. The authors attempt to bring some evi-
      dence and clarity to the similarities and differences
      between the two movements.

40   Ross, Dorothy. *G. Stanley Hall: The Psychologist as
      Prophet.* Chicago: University of Chicago Press,
      1972, 482 pp.

An extraordinary biography of the child-study
movement in America, offering a great deal of material on nineteenth century America and the roots of
developmental education. The material is a rich resource for those interested in history and the study
of the child. An extensive bibliography is included.
A comprehensive bibliography of Hall's work dating
from 1866-1923 is included.

41   Rugg, Harold. "After Three Decades of Scientific
       Method in Education", *Teachers College Record*,
       Vol. 36, No. 2, November, 1934, 111-136.

This paper was read before the National Council
of Education, February 24, 1934, by the Chairman of
the Committee on Scientific Method in Education.
It details the background and programs in the study
of education as it related to the development of a
scientific methodology. The problems involved in
integrating primary concepts from the behavioral
sciences are outlined. The conflict within disci-
plines, e.g. psychology (behaviorists and psycho-
analysts), led to difficulty in formulating a basic
methodology in education. The first three decades
of the century are seen as transition years of significance. This speech provides historical perspective to the relationship of scientific method and the
new concept of education.

42   Skidelsky, Robert. *English Progressive Schools*.
       Baltimore: Penguin Books, Inc., 1969, 272 pp.

A retrospective of the progressive movement in
England. Three major progressives, Cecil Reddie of
Abbotsholme, A. S. Neill of Summerhill, and Kurt
Hahn of Gordonstoun, are examined in terms of their
ideas and the schools in which such ideas flourished.
The material is very well presented and provides for
an in-depth look at the past with an interesting
treatment of current practices in England related
to the work of such pioneers.

43   Smith, E. Sharwood. *The Faith of a Schoolmaster*.
       London: Metheun & Company, Ltd., 1935, 253 pp.

A beautifully written work. Reflective and revealing in terms of the changes in education over a
lifetime of teaching. The forward is a stunning
educational statement. The effect of change on
teachers and pupils is intimately described.

44   Thomas, Milton and Herbert Schneider. A *Bibliography*
       of John Dewey, 1882-1939. New York: Columbia
       University Press, 1939, 246 pp.

A thorough bibliography of the work of John
Dewey. Its focus is on the philosophical works.

45   Valentine, P. F. (ed.). *Twentieth Century Education*.
      New York: Philosophical Library, 1946, 655 pp.

      A survey of educational practices and trends in
the twentieth century. The organization of the material around topics rather than years, e.g. theory,
psychology, schools, etc., is useful in providing
some integration of the historical ideas.

46   van der Eyken, William and Barry Turner. *Adventures
      in Education*. Baltimore: Penguin Books, 1975,
      190 pp.

      An examination of the innovative educational sit-
uations of the early twentieth century in England.
The Malting House School, The Burston Rebellion,
The Forest School, the work of Henry Morris, Marion
Richardson and Robin Tanner are presented within a
context of their pioneering nature and effect on
more generalized procedures in the English and American schools. The material provides needed information on this critical period of educational change.
The early work of Susan Isaacs is described in context adding material of interest to her subsequent
work. The progressive nature of these experiments
is examined within the political and social conditions of the time.

47   Ware, Caroline. *Greenwich Village: 1920-1930*.
      Boston: Houghton Mifflin Co., 1935, 496 pp.

      A sociological study of Greenwich Village, New
York City, during the twenties. This area included
a large number of immigrants as well as older New
Yorkers and bohemians. The study attempts to cover
three areas: history of the community, description
of ethnic groups, description of the institutions.
The final section includes a fine piece of reportage
on the progressive schools (City and Country, Little
Red School House and Bank Street) that were flour-
ishing at that time. A very careful study.

48   Weaver, Anthony. "Retrospect", *New Era*, Vol. 52,
      No. 7, July-August, 1971, 578-603.

      A retrospective collection of essays by leaders of
the new education: Ferriere, Neill, Rugg, Decroly,
Ensor, covering a range of topics. These essays were
originally published in the New Era during the 1920's.

49   Weber, Julia. *My Country School Diary*. New York:
     Harper and Brothers, 1946, 270 pp.

     A highly personal study documenting the author's
     life in a one-room schoolhouse. A useful addition
     to the possibilities of the educational experience
     in an active setting.

50   Wells, H. G. *The Story of a Great Schoolmaster*.
     New York: The Macmillan Company, 1924, 176 pp.

     This highly personal biography, the only one writ-
     ten by the author, of F. W. Sanderson, headmaster of
     the Oundle School, is a classic. It reveals the
     work of a progressive with singular purpose over a
     fifty-year period. Sanderson saw the school as the
     nexus for the reorganization of all civilized life
     and worked to make Oundle unique. Wells saw Sander-
     son as a practical artist of genius. The belief that
     "the whole business of life was worthwhile...through
     creative effort, through science and art and the
     school" was shared by both men. The biography gives
     substance to the life of an important progressive.

51   Wesley, E. B. *NEA: The First 100 Years*. New York:
     Harper and Company, 1957, 419 pp.

     An history of the National Educational Association
     covering the first one hundred years. Material on
     the reform and progressive movements in the context
     of large-scale organization of educators.

52   Whipple, Guy M. (ed.). *The Scientific Movement in
     Education, I and II, 37th Yearbook*. National
     Society for the Study of Education. Bloomington:
     Public School Publishing Company, 1938, 529 pp.
     each.

     These volumes represent a forty-year retrospective
     and progress report on the scientific movement in
     education. Part I deals with research and Part II
     is a review of major methodology and problem solving
     in education. Dialogue between the absolutists and
     pragmatists is contrasted in a chapter on John Dewey
     that makes for interesting speculation. These vol-
     umes help to position the work of progressive educa-
     tion in time (both philosophically and psychologic-
     ally).

Crosslistings:

     54   Baker
     59   Childs
     89   Boyd

```
101    Dewey
234    CHILDHOOD EDUCATION
328    Zirbes
347    Monroe
367    Cohen
371    Forest
398-399  Badley
403    Bourne
427    Mayhew
431    Peabody
436    Reddie
443    Washburne
444    Winsor
455-456  Mohl
```

B PHILOSOPHY

53 Archambault, Reginald (ed.). *Dewey on Education:*
    Appraisals. New York: Random House, 1966,
    235 pp.

    A collection of appraisals selected to provide a
    sense of Dewey's educational theory through time.
    Seen in terms of history, philosophy, education, and
    the future, a stimulating picture emerges providing
    impetus for further study. The essays are espec-
    ially well selected in terms of their adding to a
    cumulatively thorough and provocative portrayal of
    Dewey as educator.

54 Baker, Melvin. *Foundations of John Dewey's Educa-*
    tional Theory. New York: King's Crown Press,
    Columbia University, 1955, 214 pp.

    The development of Dewey's educational ideas are
    seen in terms of the important years between 1890-
    1904. A significant volume examining, in depth,
    Dewey's ideas on "schooling".

55 Bode, Boyd. *Progressive Education at the Crossroads*.
    New York: Newson & Company, 1938, 128 pp. (Arno
    Press, 1971, 128 pp.)

    This volume was prepared as a review of the first
    twenty years of the national progressive education
    movement and leads to an examination of the status of
    the movement within a philosophical context. A con-
    cise statement of guiding principles, problems of
    social structure and educational planning as well as
    the status of the child is set forth. A chapter on
    differences, particularly those articulated by Dr.
    Robert Hutchins, is an interesting one in terms of
    current trends. The material on Nazi Germany (Pre-
    World War II) is disturbing in light of history,
    raising new questions related to educational goals
    and the social order.

56 Branom. Mendel. *The Project Method in Education*.
    Boston: R. G. Badger, 1919, 282 pp.

An early work providing a philosophical base for the Project Method and description of its possibilities and its relationship to child growth and development. A substantive contribution to the understanding of this method. An appendix is included.

57   Chambliss, J. J. *Boyd H. Bode's Philosophy of Education.* Columbus: Phio State University Press, 1963, 98 pp.

An examination of Bode's philosophy of education based on his fashioning of pragmatism. Bode, a teacher of philosophy, moved toward a philosophy of education (1921-1944). Major interest in providing a philosophical base for educational practices. This analysis, as it relates to the progressive movement, continues to raise questions of interest in education.

58   Childs, John L. *American Pragmatism and Education.* New York: Henry Holt and Company, 1956, 373 pp.

The work of the leading educational pragmatists: Kilpatrick, Counts and Bode is examined. An historical basis (Pierce, Dewey James) is provided. This text is a careful examination of the possible directions of a pragmatic theory of education. The seriousness of the moral nature of education as it relates to democratic ideals is set forth in the final chapter.

59   Childs, John L. *Education and Morals: An Experimentalist Philosophy of Education.* New York: Appleton-Century Crofts, Inc., 1950, 299 pp.

A substantive defense of the moral foundations of democratic and experimentalist programs of education. Written after World War II, it places the earlier work of the progressive movement into perspective in terms of future educational planning. The final chapter, "The Morality of Patriotism", deals with Post-World War II conditions and provides interesting material in view of the passage of time and events.

60   Childs, John L. *Education and the Philosophy of Experimentalism.* New York: Century Company, 1931, 264 pp.

The experimentalism movement is described through a critical approach to pragmatism and progressivism. A theoretical presentation provoking questions related to the role of education. Indicates the necessary role of critical thought in educational planning. Experimentalism is seen as one of the

basic elements within the progressive movement. The
material presents the views of educationists and
examines the direction of their thinking. The forward was written by Professor Kilpatrick.

61   Cremin, Lawrence A. "John Dewey and the Progressive
        Education Movement, 1915-1952", *Teachers College
        Record*, Vol. 60, Summer, 1959,

        A pointed review of the work of Dewey as it re-
lated to the Progressive Education Movement. This
material places the thrust of Dewey's ideas into a
developmental perspective. The ideological relationship of Dewey to the movement is repeatedly clarified.

62   Curti, Merle. *The Social Ideas of American Educators*.
        Paterson: Pageant Books, 1959, 613 pp.

        The social and historical matrix within which the
leaders of the new education emerged is carefully
examined in this study. The effects of the Post-
Civil War reforms in education are seen as important
to the direction of schools in an increasingly indus-
trialized society. As prelude to the early movement
toward progressivism, the material is of more than
general interest. This work is the outcome of a
commission by the American Historical Association
Commission on the Social Studies in the Schools.
The development of social studies through an examination of the ideas of Mann, Parker, G. Stanley
Hall, William Torrey Harris, Booker T. Washington,
Dewey and others. An appended chapter brings the
material up to mid-twentieth century.

63   Darroch, Alexander. *Education and the New Utilitar-
        ianism*. London: Longman's, Green and Company,
        1914, 169 pp.

        A series of lectures by a well-known Herbartian
reflecting the main positions of the newer philosophers (Dewey, James, Croce, Bergson, Schiller) and
the ramifications of their ideas as they relate to
the schools. Some of the essays are quite dated.
The argument presented for educational evaluation of
such philosophers is cogent and provocative.

64   Dewey, John. *Democracy and Education*. New York:
        The Macmillan Company, 1916, 434 pp.

        This major work provides the reader with an intro-
duction to Dewey's philosophy of education, He relates the ideas inherent in a democratic society to
the educative process. The developments of science

and industry as they affect subject matter and
methods of instruction are carefully analyzed. Curriculum is described in some detail as it relates to
child study. Principles underlying child growth and
learning are explained. The work of the teacher in
relation to specific areas is detailed with deliber-
ate care. The primary role of experience is defined
and related to the teaching process.

65   Dewey, John. *My Pedagogic Creed*. New York: E. L.
      Kellogg & Company, 1897

      A summary of Dewey's major educational thesis and
the progressive method. A short series of five articles: What Education Is, What the School Is, The
Subject Matter of the School, The Nature of Method
and the Schools and Social Progress. This summary
provided educationists with rubrics for the "new
education". The growing sense of experimentalism
was reinforced by these articles. The social nature
of education was philosophically substantiated
throughout and a cohesive credo emerges.

66   Dewey, John. *The Quest for Certainty*. New York:
      Minton Balch & Company, 1929, 318 pp.

      An examination of the history of European philos-
ophy provides a framework for Dewey to set off his
ideas. The act of inquiry and the act of thought
are essentials of a rational approach to social
values and can provide a paradigm for education.
Education is seen in terms of learning, teaching
and morality. The ability to deal with the structuring of social values becomes a crucial dimension
of the school experience.

67   Dewey, John and John L. Childs. "The Underlying
      Philosophy in Education:, *The Educational Front-
      ier*, ed. William H. Kilpatrick, New York: The
      Century Company, 1933, 325 pp.

      The progressive ideas related to the social role
of schools, particularly in a democracy, are explic-
itly described. The relationship between the individual and society emerges as a dynamic and necessary
force moulded through schooling. The experimental
method, as a way of learning through developmental
stages, is given great importance.

68   Froebel, Friedrich. *The Education of Man*. New York:
      D. Appleton and Company, 1911, 340 pp. (Trans-
      lated and annotated by W. N. Hailmann).

      The philosophy of Friedrich Froebel is set down to
illustrate his basic principles of the educating

function of the kindergarten. Since this early work
became the hallmark for a developmental method of
education which was to influence European and American educators for the next century, it has a significant place in the literature of the progressive
period. A comprehensive look at Froebel's thoughts
and plans.

69   Horne, Herman H. *The Democratic Philosophy of Educa-
          tion: Companion to Dewey's Democracy and Educa-
          tion: Exposition and Comment.* New York: Macmil-
          lan and Company, 1932, 547 pp.

      Guide to Dewey's work with accompanying interpre-
      tations and criticism. This work reflects an analyt-
      ic and critical working through of the material in
      DEMOCRACY AND EDUCATION. An important guide to that
      work.

70   Judd, Charles. *Education and Social Progress.* New
          York: Harcourt, Brace, 1934, 286 pp.

      This volume, written by Dewey's successor at the
      University of Chicago and head of the Department of
      Education, is intended for a cultured lay audience.
      Judd calls for schools developed to provide scienti-
      fic knowledge and to facilitate the development of
      scientific method as a means of thought. He rein-
      forces those ideas of Dewey's originating at the
      Laboratory School.

71   Mort, Paul R. and William Vincent. *A Look at Our
          Schools.* New York: Cattell and Company, 1946,
          115 pp.

      A book written with a lay audience in mind. It
      is directed toward those who would like to have a
      better understanding of the philosophy and practices
      involved in the changing schools. Written by an ad-
      ministrator, attention is given to the economics and
      management of educational systems.

72   McCall, William. "My Philosophy of Life and Educa-
          tion", *Teachers College Record*, Vol. 36, Decem-
          ber, 1934, 303-314.

      A continuation and expansion of Professor McCall's
      philosophy. This paper addresses itself to the the-
      sis, "purposes should be evaluated by a really demo-
      cratic group advised by genuinely democratic experts."
      Significant questions are raised related to "Who are
      the experts?, What are their functions?. Adjustments
      of curriculum to the level of the learner is a ser-
      ious consideration. An interesting treatment of

Kendel's response to teachers as social activists in included. Professor McCall emphasizes the position of the teacher as guide.

73 Neill, A. S. *Summerhill: A Radical Approach to Child Rearing*. New York: Hart Publishing Company, Inc., 1960, 392 pp.

A. S. Neill was not a progressive in the formal sense, he was a radical innovator. However, his work should be seen in the context of progressive educational changes since it did affect both teachers and parents. Neill views education and child rearing as one. In this volume his philosophy is detailed and the plans for implementing such a philosophy are explained. Erich Fromm wrote the forward and addresses himself to the problems of freedom in education. He views Neill's work as a radical departure from that of the progressives.

74 Ratner, John (ed.). *Intelligence in the Modern World*. New York: Random House, Inc., 1939, 1077 pp.

A cooperative volume representing the range of Dewey's work in a most comprehensive manner. For the student interested in a close look at the work of Dewey this can provide a solid resource. A lengthy introduction by the editor gives shape to the work. Included are: a revised edition of HOW WE THINK, DEMOCRACY AND EDUCATION, ART AS EXPERIENCE, and the famed Kappa Delta Pi lectures.

75 Rousseau, Jean J. *Emile*. London: J. M. Dent, 1911, 444 pp.

A seminal literary work providing a basis for many of the practices espoused in the progressive movement. An attempt to show the education of the senses of Emile and Sophie as they move toward adulthood. A life-history approach to education.

76 Russell, Bertrand. *Education and the Social Order*. London: G. Allen and Unwin, Ltd., 1932, 254 pp.

Written for the layman presenting a round-up of ideas on modern changes. An anti-traditional stand is taken excepting for a new appraisal of science education. Russell, along with his wife, set up the Beacon Hill School at Petersfield as a personal laboratory for education with the goals of: courage, intelligence, sensitivity and vitality. An aesthetic sense emerges as a crucial dimension for modern man. The study of the child as a physical organism should be the beginning of the school experience.

77 Saucier, W. A. *Introduction to Modern Views of
    Education*. Chicago: Ginn and Company, 1937,
    400 pp.

    A broad view of educational problems from the
    scientific and philosophical points of view. The
    author relies strongly on the promise and proof of
    progressive education. Arguments are buttressed by
    supportive material from the Gestalt psychologists,
    environment-sociological justifications and the
    philosophy of John Dewey. An early rejection of
    I.Q. as an educational measure is declared.

78 Washburne, Carleton W. *A Living Philosophy of Educa-
    tion*. New York: The John Day Company, 1940, 585
    pp.

    The philosophical structures developed by the
    author related to children and their education within
    a democracy are revealed through experiences with
    the Winnetka Plan. A revealing source book providing
    clarification of the many practices initiated at
    Winnetka. An evaluation in some ways by one of the
    originators of this unusual community experiment
    within the public schools.

Crosslistings:

    163 Keohane
    240 Cox
    436 Reddie

C   THEORY

79   Bagley, William. *Determinism in Education*. Balti-
     more: Warwick & York, Inc., 1928, 194 pp.

     The use of a determinist theory in the develop-
     ment of educational programs is expounded.   There is
     an unusually interesting section on the I.Q. and its
     relationship to schooling in this work.

80   Bagley, William. *Education and Emergent Man*. New
     York: T. Nelson and Sons, 1934, 238 pp.

     A determinist theory of education is posited.
     The relatedness of such a theory to progressive
     education in the United States is developed.

81   Bain, Alexander. *Education as Science*. New York:
     Appleton-Century-Crofts, Inc., 1881, 453 pp.

     An early work pointing to the need for a scienti-
     fic basis for education.   This was the beginning of
     a series of books by Bain calling attention to the
     work of Herbart and the need to develop a scientific
     method of instruction.

82   Bain, Alexander. *The Senses and the Intellect*.
     London: J. W. Parker and Sons, 1894, 703 pp.

     The use of the senses in the development of in-
     tellectual faculties is postulated.   The direction
     of pedagogy moving toward a more inclusive (mind
     and body) approach to education heralds the Montes-
     sori approach and the later activity plan.

83   Bayles, Ernest. *Democratic Educational Theory*. New
     York: Harper and Brothers, 1960, 266 pp.

     This text, designed to improve educational theory,
     reflects the author's desire to draw from the past in
     as meaningful a way as possible.   The "new education"
     provides the basis of several chapters.   The problem
     of providing a theoretical framework for educational
     practices within a democracy is carefully drawn.

84 Bayles, Ernest and Bruce Hood. *Growth of American Educational Thought and Practice*. New York: Harper and Row, 1966, 305 pp.

An examination of "educational thinking" in America through a critique of practices. Excellent chapters on "Progressive Education" and "Education as Progressive Reconstruction of Experience". Sets Dewey's and Kilpatrick's differences into perspective.

85 Beck, Robert Holmes. "Progressive Education and American Progressivism", *Teachers College Record*, LX, 1958-9, 77-89, 129, 37, 190-208.

The relationship between social ideas and educational planning is clarified as the author attempts to show the inter-related aspects of educational change. The work of Felix Adler, Margaret Naumberg and Caroline Pratt is examined.

86 Benedict, Agnes. *Progress to Freedom*. New York: G. P. Putnam's Sons, 1942, 309 pp.

A sympathetic view of the progressive movement in terms of current (late 30's) practices. This material was prepared for a mass audience, particularly parents. The intention is to stimulate interest in the role of the public school in a democracy. Descriptive material of a supportive nature is used for illustrative purposes throughout. The book was written from a humanistic as well as scientific point of view. The final chapter, "Shall We Realize the Dream?" is an interesting call to action. The involvement of the handicapped in the schools and the national disinterest in education are seen as priority areas for concerned individuals.

87 Bode, Boyd. *Modern Educational Theories*. New York: The Macmillan Company, 1927, 351 pp.

A philosophical work which attempts to clarify the level of educational activity and change and, thus, orient the reader to the establishment of a position. The function of democratic processes in the formulation of a curriculum is discussed at length. A clear development of curriculum design and practices as it relates to psychological material is presented.

88 Bonser, F. G. *Life Needs and Education*. New York: Bureau of Publications, Teachers College, Columbia University, 1932, 268 pp.

The author, a professor of education at Teachers College specializing in the arts and elementary educa-

tion, has set his insights and experiences into this
volume. Some of the chapters are papers delivered
or written. "Ten Years of Progress in Elementary
Education" is an examination of the progressive movement in the second decade of the century. Development of a thesis that focuses on life experiences
used within the school as a "means of enlarging life".
A substantive work on the life/educational cycle.
Includes bibliography on curriculum making.

89   Boyd, William. *From Locke to Montessori*. London:
      George G. Harrap & Company, 1914, 271 pp.

      A critical approach to the Montessori point of
view through an analysis of its philosophical implications. Historical references are made in chapters
related to Locke, Condillac, Pereira, Rousseau, Itard
and Sequin. The "omission of the humanistic subjects" provides material on educational dissonance
(questions related to the role of early school situations vis-a-vis the home are pursued). A Marxist
view is promulgated.

90   Boyd, William. *Educational Movements and Methods*.
      Boston: D. C. Heath and Company, 1924, 189 pp.

      A round-up volume on current (1920's) practices.
The work of Parkhurst and Montessori are given interesting treatment. The Heuristic method is analyzed. A chapter on intelligence testing in the newer
settings is particularly interesting.

91   Breed, Frederick. "What is Progressive Education?",
      Elementary Journal, (October, 1933), Vol. XXXIV,
      No. 2, 111-117.

      A critical analysis of theories of selected lead-
ers in progressive education. Raising several timely
questions related to objectives and process.

92   Brim, Orville. *The Foundations of Progressive Educa-
      tion*. Columbus: Ohio State University Press,
      1935, 17 pp.

      A paper presented to the Elementary Education Club
at Ohio State stating the rationale and need for a
re-examination of the movement in terms of the establishment of a foundation. The behavioral science approach to the activity programs and certain practices
and principles of the movement is highlighted through
references to the work of Lashley, Jennings, Taba and
Coghill.

93 Childs, John L. and William H. Kilpatrick. *John
    Dewey as Educator: Two Essays.* New York: Pro-
    gressive Education Association, 1939.

These two essays were reprinted by the Association
from Volume One: The Philosophy of John Dewey. "The
Educational Philosophy of John Dewey" by Professor
Childs presents the experimental aspects involved in
education as it relates to experience and interaction
of the individual. The social dimensions of the individual's needs and society's needs are examined.
The current state of democracy as viewed by Dewey
emerges in both essays. The second essay, "Dewey's
influence on Education" by Professor Kilpatrick provides an analysis of the philosophical ideas as they
moved into the practical arena of curriculum and
schools.

94 Cobb, Stanwood. *New Horizons for the Child.* Wash-
    ington, D. C.: The Avalon Press, 1934, 212 pp.

A plea for the new education by the founder of the
Progressive Education Association. The widening
basis of the new social order that requires a different look at educational goals is developed. A highly
personal view. The appendix includes poems from second and third graders at the famed Chevy Chase Country Day School.

95 Cobb, Stanwood. *The New Leaven.* New York: The John
    Day Company, 1928, 340 pp.

A homely and warm book reflecting the author's
wide vista of the movement. As founder of the Progressive Education Association in 1919 and later
president, the views indicate his partiality. The
sub-title for this work is "Progressive Education and
its Effect Upon the Child and Society". Drawing on
his experiences including his founding of the Chevy
Chase Country Day School a framework is provided that
reveals a rich panorama of children, parents, teachers and administrators engaged in the movement. Specific case studies are presented. An indictment of
the secondary schools and college curriculums is made.

96 Cole, Percival R. *Herbart and Froebel: An Attempt
    at Synthesis.* New York: Teachers College,
    Columbia University, 1907, 116 pp.

A slender volume that brings the work of Froebel
and Herbart into very sharp focus. Through an analysis of the philosophical structures and principles
of both men, a synthesis is attempted. The relationship of kindergarten to primary education is given as

a rationale or need for such a synthesis. The interplay between activity of the child and teacher-directed activity is interesting.

97   Counts, George S. *Education and the Promise of America*. New York: The Macmillan Company, 1946, 157 pp.

This seventeenth volume of the Kappa Delta Pi Lecture Series is both a retrospective and future view of American education. The author, a spokesman for the "new education" discusses the effects of technological and sociological change on the schools. This is a general statement structured about a series of postulates. It is also a call for comprehensive vocational training.

98   Cubberly, Ellwood P. *Changing Conception of Education*. Boston: Houghton Mifflin, 1909, 67 pp.

An early review of the movement toward a more scientific view of education and the need to move toward an awareness of increased industrialization as an educational need.

99   Dell, Floyd. *Were You Ever a Child?* New York: Alfred A. Knopf, 1919, 202 pp.

An unusual review of educational practices and the relationship of newer discoveries in the behavioral sciences (circa 1900-1915). The needs of the twentieth century are described and one chapter is devoted to the future: "Education in 1947 A.D." is fascinating current reading. Problems related to the nature of the child and the nature of modern life are examined in a lively and provocative manner. Chapters are brief and refreshingly shorn of any pedantry, unusual for this period.

100   Dewey, John et al. *Art and Education*. Merion, Pa.: Barnes Foundation Press, 1969, 3rd Edition, 316 pp.

The striking collaboration of Dewey and A. S. Barnes resulted in a major contribution related to art education. Dewey, in the preface, indicates his pleasure in the application of his ideas related to thought and education through the work of the Barnes Foundation in aesthetic education. A broad range of essays (some by Dewey) on thinking, art and education are very stimulating. A chapter, "Sabotage of Public Education in Philadelphia", is a particularly interesting insight into the dynamic quality of this collaboration.

101 Dewey, John. *Education Today*. New York: G. P. Putnam and Sons, Co., 1940, 165 pp.

A review of education from 1900-1940 in a series
of forty-five essays. A wide range is covered and
the material forms an interesting historical view of
Dewey's thoughts.

102 Dewey, John. *Experience and Education*. New York:
The Macmillan Company, 1938, 116 pp.

A re-evaluation and, to some extent, a reitera-
tion of earlier ideas in light of the expressed need
of Dewey to focus on change rather than the solidi-
fication of the movement within a single ideology.

103 Dewey, John. "Historical Developments of Invention
and Occupation, Central Principles", *Elementary
School Record*, 1900.

A particularly useful article as it places Montessori and Dewey as fellow travelers. The exposition and unifying principles that the child can re-
spond to is of more than historical value. The need
for child-directed activities is related to learning
and thought processes.

104 Dewey, John. *How We Think*. Boston: D. C. Heath
and Company, 1916, 301 pp.

The act of thought is analyzed and discussed in
terms of Dewey's conceptualization of scientific
method. The sub-title clarifies the position taken
by Dewey vis-a-vis schooling, "A Restatement of the
Relation of Reflective Thinking to the Educative
Process". A seminal work in which thought becomes
an outcome of the educative process. The relationship of texts, experience, play, language, observation and recording of data and phenomena is examined.
The interplay of conscious and unconscious processes
in thought are described. The development of a five-
step sequence for problem solving in terms of thinking is Dewey's substitute for Herbart's five teaching
steps.

105 Dewey, John. "Significance of the School of Education", *The Elementary School Teacher*, March,
1904.

An address given by Professor Dewey at a meeting
of the schools assembled into the School of Education
at the University of Chicago. The idea of co-educa-
tion between teachers, parents, and children is presented. The problems of amalgamating the practical

and the abstract in teaching and learning is set forth with some strength.

106 Dworkin, Martin S. *Dewey on Education*. New York: Teachers College, Columbia University, 1959, 134 pp.

A useful compendium guide to Dewey's PROGRESSIVE EDUCATION AND THE SCIENCE OF EDUCATION, MY PEDAGOGIC CREED and THE CURRICULUM. Annotations and discussion to the texts are lively.

107 Everett, Samuel. *Democracy Faces the Future*. New York: Columbia University Press, 1935, 269 pp.

A survey of thinking on social, economic and political problems of the times (1930's). Particular emphasis on the status, role and future of progressive education and progressive educators provides currently interesting material. Chapter bibliographic notes are lengthy and informative.

108 Feinberg, Walter. "Progressive Education and Social Planning", *Teachers College Record*, Vol. 73, No. 4, May, 1972, 485-506.

The improvement of current school systems and programs can be effected through an examination of past practices, particularly those of the progressives as viewed by the author.

109 Gerwig, George W. *Schools With a Perfect Score*. New York: The Macmillan Company, 1918, 194 pp.

A call for schools that will help "make democracy safe for the world...". This unusual book, written by the Secretary to the Board of Public Education in Pittsburgh, Pennsylvania, presents a clear statement of reasons for upgrading school systems. A report card listing seven givens precedes the text and makes for interesting assessment criteria. The need to obtain perfection for the public schools is considered crucial to the survival of democracy. Such socio-educational statements helped to bring the progressive message to the attention of both educators and the public.

110 Gesell, Arnold. *The Guidance of Mental Growth in Infant and Child*. New York: The Macmillan Company, 1930, 322 pp.

A response to the rapid development of pre-school programs and interest in the young child. This volume indicates, with clarity and insight, the role of the home and the school in the development of the child. Material on the "new role" of the kindergarten indicates the usefulness of the progressives in planning programs. An influential book in its time.

111 Gesell, Arnold. *The Mental Growth of the Pre-School Child.* New York: The Macmillan Company, 1925, 447 pp.

A basic text used by early childhood educators on the mental development of the young child (0-6 years). A system of developmental diagnosis is carefully developed and presented. Richly illustrated with photographs.

112 Giles, Harry H. *Teacher-Pupil Planning.* New York: Harper & Brothers, 1941, 395 pp.

This suggestive text covers those aspects of operative activity related to planning for learning. A definition of terms, clarification of the problems posed and management of an environment for such democratic action is detailed. The second half provides a series of illustrative cases from a wide range of schools. Junior high and senior high school grades are included. This material is in narrative form and illuminates the material in the first section. A bibliography is included. Classroom democracy as a necessary requirement in preparing children to become active, participating citizens in a democracy is the central theme.

113 Hamaide, Amelie. *The DeCroly Class.* New York: E. P. Dutton and Company, 1924, 318 pp. (Translated by J. L. Hunt)

The DeCroly Method was used in many music programs in the more progressive schools. This text is a basic reference work explaining its history, theory and the techniques used in classrooms with children. The introduction by Claparede is particularly interesting. DeCroly collaborated with the author in the preparation of this text.

114 Hart, Joseph Kimmont. *A Social Interpretation of Education.* New York: Henry Holt and Company, 1929, 458 pp.

An analysis of the new trend in education as a reflection of social change, scientific discoveries and economic needs. Contrasts between "old schools" and "new schools" are frequently made. This volume places the movement into social, educational and psychological focus. Interesting questions are raised through the material in the lengthy and well-organized index.

115   Herbart, Johann F. *Outlines of Educational Doctrine.*
      New York: The Macmillan Company, 1901, 334 pp.
      (Translated by A. E. Large)

      A comprehensive view of the ideas and principles
      underlying the Herbartian approach to education.
      This volume represents the author"s working princi-
      ples as they related to specific teaching techniques.
      The role of the teacher in the learning of the child
      is carefully described. An influential book in its
      time.

116   Herbart, Johann F. *The Science of Education.*
      Boston: D. C. Heath & Company, 1902, 308 pp.
      (Translated by H. & E. Flekin)

      This seminal work brings the original thinking of
      Herbart in relationship to the development of a
      pedagogy based on scientific principles. The five
      part lesson or learning possibility available to
      teachers became the guideline in teacher training
      institutions for classroom instruction until Dewey
      attacked it as teacher centered and teacher-goal
      oriented. It was a model of the breaking down of
      the teaching task into elements that were describable
      and even quantifiable in terms of measurement and
      evaluation.

117   Hissong, Clyde. *The Activity Movement.* Baltimore:
      Warwick & York, Inc., 1932, 122 pp.

      A study reflecting the author's interest in dis-
      covering the principles of the movement. An inves-
      tigation of the influence of traditional concepts
      related to the development of the movement and to
      correlate such findings with knowledge of child
      development. An emphasis on biological foundations
      provides for a chapter on genetics and environment.
      The author was a student of Boyd Bode and O. G.
      Brim; their influence is evident in the comclusions
      reached. The limitations of the practices are de-
      scribed and suggestions made related to future cur-
      riculum development.

118   Isaacs, Susan. *Social Development in the Young
      Child.* London: Routledge & Kegan Paul, 1933,
      480 pp.

      A companion volume to INTELLECTUAL GROWTH IN
      YOUNG CHILDREN. This work, drawn from the author's
      experiences with the Malting House studies at Cam-

bridge, focuses upon the social nature of child development. Children's movement toward social control and activities through which socialization progresses are developed and examined. A pioneering effort in the area of child study and development. The progressive and the kindergarten movements relied heavily on the data presented for curriculum design and direction.

119 Isaacs, Susan. *Intellectual Growth in Young Children*. New York: Schocken Paperback, 1968, 295 pp.

The companion volume to SOCIAL DEVELOPMENT IN YOUNG CHILDREN presents records of the work of children at the Malting House School, Cambridge. Discovery, reasoning and thought are the areas covered in detail. The material is drawn from experiences with Geoffrey and Margaret Pyke. A pioneering work in the area of child study and development as it directly relates to designing and directing educational experiences.

120 Kelley, Earl C. *Education for What is Real*. New York: Harper and Brothers, 1947, 114 pp.

The introduction by John Dewey notes the experimental work by Dr. Ames at the Hanover Institute related to perception. Kelley reports on the importance to educators of Ames' work by discussing the findings of the research at the Institute (formerly the Dartmouth Eye Institute) and his ten-week visit there. Kelley sees perception as the basis of knowing. The experimental factor in learning becomes the critical dimension for both teaching and learning. Curriculum that is static is seen as self-defeating. The text is an attempt to interpret scientific findings in terms of educational possibilities.

121 Kilpatrick, William Heard. *Education for a Changing Civilization*. New York: The Macmillan Company, 1931, 143 pp.

A series of three lectures delivered at Rutgers University in 1926 for the Kellogg Foundation. The theme is change. The nature of change, the demands of education and the results of rapid change on education are developed. Weight is placed on a new conceptualization of curriculum to provide for successful school experiences designed to being about a reconstruction of experience for the child. This change is mediated by the loss of relevance in the teacher-learner relationship. A more radical view of teachers is presented in which teachers are seen

as making themselves obsolete if the educational process is to be considered a success.

122 Kilpatrick, William Heard. *Philosophy of Education*.
     New York: The Macmillan Company, 1951, 465 pp.

     A comprehensive volume of the author's analysis of
     the principle problems of contemporary general educa-
     tional theory. The book is not centered on the pro-
     gressive movement. However, the full range of the
     author's views and theories related to the education-
     al process is made available. Since he was so import-
     ant a figure in the movement, this later work is a
     valuable document.

123 Kilpatrick, William Heard. "Recent Psychological
     Developments: What They Mean for Curriculum
     Making", *Journal of the National Education
     Association*, Vol. 24, December, 1935, 277-282.

     Kilpatrick draws on the shifts in psychology and
     the focus on the individual and his development to
     make a case for changes in the directions being fol-
     lowed in curriculum making. The problems of group
     instruction versus individual instruction is not
     clarified. However, the use of current views in
     psychology by Kilpatrick is of interest.

124 Kilpatrick, William Heard. "What Do We Mean By
     Progressive Education?", *Progressive Education*,
     VII, No. 8, Dec., 1930, 383-386.

     A radio series on progressive education included
     this talk by the author. A brisk over-view of the
     basis and goals of progressive education is provided.
     Comparison between traditional and newer schools is
     made. The talk is of interest since it was directed
     to a mass audience via the medium of radio.

125 Kirkpatrick, E. A. *Fundamentals of Child Study*.
     New York: The Macmillan Company, 1917, 380 pp.

     Early work in child study focusing on the senses
     and instincts.

126 Lane, Robert H. *The Progressive Elementary School*.
     New York: Houghton Mifflin Company, 1938, 266 pp.

     The philosophical ideas inherent in progressive
     education are placed into a theoretical construct.
     This theory is then applied to its function within an
     elementary school. Through discussion of the prob-
     lems with progressive educational practices and be-
     liefs, the author attempts to bring "light" to both

an academic audience and to parents in a straight-
forward text.

127 Langford, Howard. *Education and Social Conflict*.
     New York: The Macmillan Company, 1936, 210 pp.

     An evaluation of the requirements of a social
     state. Indications that such a state necessitates
     changes, reinforced the ideas of the progressives
     that the schools can affect large-scale change. The
     gap between theory and practice within the progressive
     movement is critically approached. The criticism is
     of a constructive nature.

128 Lay, Wilhelm August. *Experimental Pedagogy with
     Particular Reference to Education Through Activ-
     ity*. New York: Prentice-Hall, 1936, 371 pp.

     A sizable text translated from the German by
     Adolph Weil of the work of Wilhelm Lay. Fascinating
     material on educational psychology is to be found
     within this older classic: effects of time of day
     on students' performances, facial gestures and pos-
     ture in relation to learning, etc. The organic cur-
     riculum is promoted and carefully explained.

129 Maritain, Jacques. *Education at the Crossroads*.
     New Haven: Yale University Press, Inc., 1934,
     120 pp.

     A printing of the Terry Lectures delivered by
     Maritain at Yale University in 1943. These lectures
     reflect on the aims and dynamics of education. Pro-
     fessor Maritain attempts to bring the relationship
     of the humanities and liberal education into focus.
     Citing the situation in wartime Europe, he calls for
     a new look at the pragmatic trend of the progressives.
     His comments on Dewey are indirect but identifiable.

130 Mirick, George. *Progressive Education*. New York:
     Houghton Mifflin Company, 1923, 314 pp.

     A basic text on newer classroom practices and
     possibilities including project work. A definition
     of the new movement is developed throughout.

131 Montessori, Maria. *Education for a New World*.
     Madras, India: Kalakohctra Publications, 1946,
     89 pp.

     A short text on the nature of the childs develop-
     mental needs related to education and the social
     character of the emerging person. Montessori reflected
     the concern and overwhelming need to deal with the

real world of the present in the education of the
growing child in this volume. Her faith in a scientific basis for educational practices is reaffirmed
throughout.

132 Montessori, Maria. *The "Erdkinder" and the Functions
     of the University*. Amsterdam: The Association
     Montessori Internationale, n.d., 32 pp.

Two papers dealing with Montessori's ideas on reform in education during and after the adolescent
period. Both of these papers permit the reader to
better understand the global aspect of the Montessori plan of education following the developmental
needs of the child. Moral and social development is
considered in both papers. The material on boarding
schools is of interest. Some of the reforms discussed are reflected in the work of American reformers during the progressive era between the wars.

133 Montessori, Maria. *Pedagogical Anthropology*. New
     York: Frederick A. Stokes Company, 1913, 508 pp.
     (Translated by F. T. Cooper)

This early work of Montessori's sets forth her
ideas and theories related to a scientific approach
to education. The early sense of methodology de-
rived from scientific method are elaborated. The
development of the intellect is postulated in terms
of a parallel between that of the historical development of man. Based on a series of lectures given at
the University of Rome over a four year period. The
influence of Darwin appears as a strong element in
the development of her ideas.

134 McGregor, A. L. *The Junior High School Teacher*.
     New York: Doubleday, Doran, 1929, 284 pp.

The relationship between student and teacher in
this emerging "bridge" school, the "junior high", is
detailed as the author describes the opportunities
to be found in such a setting. The quality of
change for both student and teachers in this setting
is seen as a very positive one.

135 Naumberg, Margaret. *The Child and the World*. New
     York: Harcourt, Brace and Company, 1928, 328 pp.

The founder of the Walden School, New York City,
sets forth her philosophy of education through a
series of dialogues. The fourteen dialogues represent a range of views: school superintendents,
sociologist, artist, students, parents, physician,
university professor and stage producer. Each dia-

logue attempts to bring new light to a view of education and the child. A great deal is covered in this
volume. The discussions are structured and collect-
ively provide a gestalt representing a scientific
and progressive approach to education.

136 Neill, A. S. *Freedom---Not License*. New York: Hart
     Publishing Company, Inc., 1966, 192 pp.

     A follow-up volume to SUMMERHILL. This text at-
     tempts to clarify the difference between freedom and
     license as it relates to the total education of the
     child. The emphasis is on the child in the American
     home. The collision of a permissive environment with
     the developmental needs of a child are described in
     such a way that the relationship to school life is
     clarified.

137 Parker, Francis. *Talks on Pedagogics: An Outline
     on the Theory of Concentration*. New York: The
     John Day Campany (revised edition), 1931, 491 pp.

     A revised edition of "talks" given at the Teach-
     er's Retreat, Chataqua Assembly, New York (1891) by
     Colonel Parker. The theory of concentration devel-
     oped by Parker as a means of better understanding the
     study of education as a science is expanded and an
     analysis of attention, observation and reading is
     provided.

138 Radich, Sheila. *The New Children: Talks With Dr.
     Maria Montessori*. New York: Frederick A. Stokes
     Company, 1920, 168 pp.

     An exciting collection of conversations and
     thoughts first published as a magazine series. An
     attempt to clarify questions related to Montessori's
     ideas and practices. The author, interested in the
     work of Jung (psychology) and Bergson (philosophy),
     sees an integration of their work for education in
     the ideas of Montessori.

139 Rainwater, Clarence. *The Play Movement in the United
     States*. Chicago: The University of Chicago Press,
     1922, 371 pp.

     An historical and analytic study of the Play Move-
     ment through an examination of current (1920) methods
     and past practices and procedures. This early work,
     undertaken in Chicago, seriously effected the plan-
     ning of the newer educational programs.

140 Rank, Otto. *Modern Education*. New York: Alfred A.
     Knopf, Inc., 1932, 243 pp.

A lost book. This volume brings the relationship of the then new field of psychoanalysis into close contact with the education of the child. A call to understand the needs of the developing person through the educational experience which should include the field of psychoanalysis. The problems involved in a socially proscribed and directed education are particularly relevant to progressive educational goals.

141 Robbins, C. I. *An Introduction to the Study of Social Education*. New York: Allyn & Bacon, 1918, 470 pp.

An early book directed to the view that schools are social institutions. This view is discussed in terms of the changing role for the school, namely as the instrument of progress within a society. The type of curriculum that should be studied in such institutions is presented as well as the role of the teacher in socialization. The material reflects the concern for the role schools should play in a dynamic democracy. A re-definition of educational goals is called for based on a social view.

142 Rugg, Harold. *Foundation of American Education*. New York: World Book Company, Inc., 1947, 826 pp.

The effect of the progressive movement as it related to larger societal changes' impact on education. Particular emphasis is placed on the thrust of curriculum at the elementary and secondary levels in terms of setting educational objectives and practices and obtaining such goals. Viewed from the position of leadership in this educational shift, the material is tightly focused on the progressive view. The need for an integration of sociology, psychology, economics and philosophy in educational thought.

143 Schoenchen, Gustav G. *The Activity School*. London: Longmans, Green, 1941, 359 pp.

A treatise on the work of the Austrian student of educational theory, Edoard Burger. A basic philosophical work for teachers recounting the ideas of Comenius, Froebel, Rousseau and Herbart and relating such work to the idea of schools based on integrated activity. An important seminal work.

144 Stevenson, John A. *The Project Method of Teaching*. New York: The Macmillan Company, 1925, 305 pp.

This early work on the project method is an attempt to place the theoretical structure undergirding this teaching technique within the context of classroom programming. A clear statement.

145   Thorndike, E. L. *The Principles of Teaching Based on Psychology*. New York: A. G. Seiler, 1906, 177 pp.

An early work on pedagogy stressing the need to fuse the newer scientific approach with current practices. Edward Lee Thorndike was to be a strong influencer of the direction of much research undertaken during the progressive period.

146   Washburne, Carleton W. *What Is Progressive Education?* New York: The John Day Company, 1952, 155 pp.

A simple statement of the need for change in schools and a justification of the methods involved in progressive education. Individual growth possibilities within such a setting is developed by one of the leaders in the movement. This book, published toward the end of Washburne's career, was written especially for the lay person, particularly the parent who would like to know more about the progressive movement. It is clear, concise and convincing in its thrust.

147   Washburne, Carleton, C. W. and Myron Stearns. *Better Schools*. New York: The John Day Company, 1928, 342 pp.

A highly interesting critique and call for education that can improve the lives of children and the communities in which they live. The need for change and descriptions of possibilities to effect such change in classrooms and schools provides interesting material for administrators and teachers.

148   Wilson, H. and G. M. Wilson. *The Motivation of School Work*. Boston: Houghton Mifflin Company, 1916, 265 pp.

An early work on motivation as an integral element in learning. Through an analysis of current (1910) needs in education the author provides a framework for future activity programs. An interesting insight into the rationale for the activity method.

149   Zachry, Caroline. "Mental Hygiene and Classroom Procedures", *NEA Journal*, Vol. 20, October, 1931, pp. 243-244.

A concise over-view of the mental health requirements of children in schools. The role schools and

teachers can take in a progressive setting is clarified. Comparison of ways in which traditional and
progressive settings meet such needs is described.

150   Zepper, John T. "Krupskaya on Dewey's Educational
      Thought", *School and Society*, Vol. 100, No.
      2338, January, 1972, 19-21.

      Lenin's wife, Krupskaya, was an ardent advocate of
Dewey in the Soviet Union. This article examines
her writings related to Dewey and progressive education and attempts to relate such work to the development of Marxian education.

Crosslistings:

      179   Beck
      189   Demashkevich
      217   Bagley
      218   Bain
      223   Blow
      227   Bonser
      228   Boyd
      239   Cook
      244   Dalcroze
      246-247 Dewey
      280-281 Mearns
      290-291 Montessori
      302   Patty
      307   Slavson
      330   Burton
      338   Kandel
      341   Kilpatrick
      348-349 Montessori
      409   Curry
      423   Isaacs

D COMPARATIVE

151 Alexander, Thomas and Beryl Parker. *The New Education in the German Republic.* New York: The John
Day Company, 1939, 387 pp.

A descriptive accounting based on visitations to
a range of educational facilities from hostels
through the universities in Nazi Germany. The New
Order is praised and supported by the authors with
particular praise for the Youth Movement. A particularly interesting book in light of the history of
the thirties and forties. Educational reform was
seen as a strong force in Germany at this time. English and American reformers were impressed and in-
fluenced by the changes. Kandel's THE MAKING OF
NAZIS brings the role of the new education in Pre-
World War II Germany into sharp focus and provides a
contrasting view.

152 Ash, Maurice, et al. *Who Are the Progressives Now?*
London: Routledge & Kegan Paul, 1969, 253 pp.

A lively collection taken from the Dartington
Colloquoy of April, 1965. The first part of the
book deals with the nature of conflict between the
classical progressives and the modernists. An accounting of the progressive movement in England.
Part Two provides extracts from papers selected to
represent divergent views. English progressive
schools differed from those in the United States.
Evaluations of past programs are described. An
"appendix" on creativity as a function of the type
of education reports with thoroughness the results
of testing to determine the differences among children with varied educational experiences.

153 Cusden, Phoebe. *The English Nursery School.* London:
Kegan Paul, Trench, Trueber & Co., Ltd., 1938,
290 pp.

A survey of the historical background of the nursery movement in England. The relationship between
the movement in the United States and England is est-

ablished. Detailed material on the content and practices of nursery schools is included.

154 Dottrens, Robert, in *The New Education in Austria*.
ed. Paul Dengler. New York: The John Day Company, 1930, 226 pp.

A detailed account of the change in Austrian
educational planning. The description of the basic
formulations of the new education are interesting
when contrasted with the work in the United States.
Teacher training and school administration within
the framework of new goals is carefully presented
and interesting.

155 Fediaevsky, Vera and Patty Smith Hill. *Nursery
School and Parent Education in Soviet Russia*.
New York: E. P. Dutton & Co., 1936, 265 pp.

The extensive area of nursery education in the
Soviet Union is covered through text and photographs.
The relationship of medical and social services to
this period of growth and education is detailed. The
author, a leader in Soviet pre-school education, has
provided an inclusive view of the toys, equipment,
programs, routines and parent education sessions.
The collaboration of Patty Smith Hill helps to bring
the practices into the purvue of the American reader.

156 Ferriere, Adolphe. *The Activity School*. New York:
The John Day Company, 1927, 339 pp.

A translation (by F. Dean Moore and F. C. Wooten)
of the major work of Dr. Ferriere of the Jean Jacques
Rousseau Institute at Geneva. This book brought
European ideas on progressive education to Americans.
The psychological basis for activity-oriented programs of education is presented. The developmental
aspects of child growth and educational practices
are described in terms of manual, social, and intellectual activity. A schematic of the formation
of psychological types is particularly interesting
in light of Piagetian theory.

157 Grant, Cecil. *English Education and Dr. Montessori*.
London: Wells, Gardner, Darton & Company, Ltd.,
1913, 105 pp.

An examination of the theory and philosophy of
Dr. Montessori. The implications of her work in
terms of future changes in the systems of education
are suggested. Discussion of visits to schools in
Italy and the questions raised by observers are
presented in terms of Montessori as a progressive
theorist whose work relates to the "new education".

158 Holmes, Harry E. "Bolshevik Utilitarianism and
    Educational Experimentalism: Past Attitudes
    and Soviet Educational Practice, 1917-1931",
    History of Education Quarterly, Vol. 13, No. 4,
    Winter, 1973, 347-365.

    An excellent round-up review of the influence of
    Montessori, Parkhurst, Dewey and the progressive
    movement on the Soviet educational system. The
    changes during the twenties in Russia are seen in
    terms of the political and economic climate in which
    educational change occurred.

159 Institution: The Children's Friends. *A Key to the
    Heart of the Child*. Amsterdam: The Children's
    Friends, 1937, 197 pp.

    The report of a commission by the municipality of
    Amsterdam to study character development and practi-
    cal education in the United States and other coun-
    tries. Comparative data was sought on programs, bud-
    gets, curriculum and school plants. Interviews with
    educators (Collegiate, Lincoln, Corpus Christi and
    selected public schools in New York City and neigh-
    boring suburbs, as well as Merrill Palmer, Detroit,
    and European and African schools). The material is
    descriptive and schools can be compared to their of-
    ferings and philosophy; an unusual text.

160 Kandel, I. L. *The Making of Nazis*. New York:
    Bureau of Publications, Teachers College, Colum-
    bia University, 1935, 138 pp.

    This volume, written before the Alexander and
    Parker text on the NEW EDUCATION IN THE GERMAN RE-
    PUBLIC, is a sobering statement on the problems in-
    herent in social uses of education. The conflict be-
    tween democracy and totalitarianism is seen as a
    critical one when translated into educational aims.

161 Kandel, I. L. *The New Era in Education: A Compara-
    tive Study*. Boston: Houghton Mifflin Company,
    1955, 388 pp.

    International current trends in education, influ-
    ences, leaders and educational practices are exam-
    ined through this comparative study. The function
    of education in societies, the role taken by educa-
    tors and the patterns of educational organization
    are detailed. Educational practices related to pre-
    school children, primary and adolescent children are
    viewed within a comparative framework. Teacher
    training and certification procedures are revealing.

162 Keohane, Mary. "A. S. Neill: Latter Day Dewey?",
    Elementary School Journal, Vol. 70, No. 8, May,
    1970, 401-410.

    A comparison of the philosophies of John Dewey
    and A. S. Neill. Both men are seen as progressives
    and commonalities in their ideas are discussed as
    well as examination of differences.

163 McLear, Martha. *The Kindergarten and the Montessori
    Method: An Attempt at Synthesis*. Boston: Rich-
    ard G. Badger, 1914, 114 pp.

    An attempt to evaluate European Montessori prac-
    tices in terms of the needs and expectations of the
    American kindergarten. The author, a professor of
    education at Howard University, attempts to clarify
    some of the more controversal aspects of the Montes-
    sori practices. A child development point of view
    is the basis for synthesis. A curious letter from
    G. Stanley Hall precedes the text.

164 Makarenko, A. *Problems of Soviet School Education*.
    Moscow: Progress Publishers, 1965, 154 pp.

    The view of a new education based on a redefini-
    tion of discipline is provided by a leading "new"
    educator. The child study approach is adapted to
    collective education. The craftsmanship of teaching
    towards these newer goals is detailed: "a faculty
    for quiet orientation, self-control, calm, confi-
    dence, and an ability to influence effectively not
    just the collective...but every one of its members
    taken separately". A series of lectures given for
    teachers by an influential Russian.

165 Marraro, Howard. *The New Education in Italy*. New
    York: S. F. Vanni, Inc., 1936, 506 pp.

    A comprehensive pro-fascist view of changes in
    Italian education from nursery through the univer-
    sity. The reforms of Gentile at the elementary level
    are described and help to explain the differences be-
    tween elementary and secondary goals. Programs of
    study are included. A criticism of these reforms
    comprise one chapter. A bibliography is included.

166 Meyer, Adolphe. *Public Education in Modern Europe*.
    New York: Avon Press, 1928, 262 pp.

    An objective and descriptive work on the state of
    education in public schools in selected countries of
    Europe: England, France, Italy, Russia and Germany.
    A report on the pre and post World War conditions of
    public education.

167 Minio-Palvello, L. *Education in Facist Italy*. New
     York: Oxford University Press, 1946, 236 pp.

     An unusual book written during the fascist regime
     in Italy. Describes history, state of schools, and
     changes during this period of social change. The
     work of the Minister of Education, Bottai, is dis-
     cussed in terms of his attempt to both humanize and
     articulate the curriculum at varying levels. The
     new humanism emerges as an important dimension in
     the changes in the educational system during this
     period.

168 Roman, Frederick W. *The New Education in Europe*.
     New York: E. P. Dutton & Company, Inc., 1923,
     271 pp., rev. ed. 1930 (enlarged), 423 pp.

     Written after World War I, education is viewed as
     a necessary tool in the prevention of future wars.
     School reform in Europe and Great Britain is exam-
     ined. The role of the new education in such reform
     is described for several countries.

169 Sizer, Nancy F. *Dewey, China and the Philosophy of
     Development: A Contrast of American Progressive
     Educational Thought and Practice With That of
     Modern China*. ERIC, 1974, 24 pp.

     A report in the form of an address of Dewey's in-
     fluence on modern education in China. The results
     of Dewey's two year visit to China after World War
     I are discussed and the ramifications of his ideas
     on the educational planning and practices in China
     are described with some detail.

170 Snell, Reginald. *Progressive Schools: Their Prin-
     ciples and Practice*. London: Hogarth Press,
     1934, 197 pp.

     An examination of the English progressive school,
     particularly during the twenties. Virginia Woolf and
     L. B. Pekin are called on for comments and the mater-
     ial is particularly interesting in terms of the
     British approach to change.

171 Specht, Minna and A. Rosenberg. *Experimental Schools
     in Germany*. London: German Educational Recon-
     structionists, 1945, 37 pp.

     A short work describing a dozen experimental
     schools in Germany from 1897. An interesting col-
     lection from Herman Leitz to the Hamburg Community
     Schools. The new education's position vis-a-vis the
     emerging political thrust (Nazism) is discussed. A

valuable reading for those interested in the political ramifications of educational change.

172 Stewart, William A. C. *Progressives and Radicals in English Education, 1750-1970*. New Jersey: A. M. Kelley, 1972, 529 pp.

The second half of this volume deals with the twentieth century. An extensive view is provided of this period. The work of Neill, Montessori, Badley, Steiner and Reddie is placed into historical perspective. The influence of the new psychology on the direction of educational changes emerges as a dynamic force.

173 Stuerm, Francis. *Training in Democracy*. New York: Inor Publishing Company, 1938, 256 pp.

A view of the new education in Czeckoslovokia provides material on the changes taking place and the implementation of wide-spread reorganization of curriculum at all levels.

174 Washburne, Carleton and Myron Stearns. *New Schools in the Old World*. New York: The John Day Company, 1926, 174 pp.

A sympathetic and emotional critique by the superintendent of the Winnetka Public Schools of a dozen European progressive schools. The selectiveness of the schools visited ranges from schools for young children to older children in residential settings to handicapped children. Eight countries are included and schools involved in Montessori, DeCroly, Cousinet instruction are represented. The book is easily read and represents the insights and questions of an American educator interested in the relevance of methods observed abroad in the light of American needs with particular emphasis on individualization of instruction.

175 White, Jessie. *Montessori Schools*. Oxford: Horace Hart, 1913, 185 pp.

A personal account of two month's observations at the Montessori schools in Milan, Verona and Rome, Italy, during 1913. Descriptive and critical material on a dozen schools by an English educationist. Commentary on the use of materials by children. The variations in the programs and practices are described and discussed, An interesting volume written with objectivity.

176 Wright, Bernard. *Educational Heresies*. London:
     Noel Douglas, 1925, 136 pp.

     A lively view of educational needs and practices
seen through the eyes of an Englishman. The author
provides critical analysis of many of the contemporary and modern views of education including the Gary
School Experiment in Gary, Indiana. Some surprising
material is found in the commentary.

Crosslistings:

     55   Bode
     189 Demashkevich
     228 Boyd

E CRITICISM

177 Bantock, G. H. *Education and Values*. London:
Faber and Faber, 1965, 182 pp.

A contemporary re-evaluation of early "scientific"
educators. An examination of the thrust of sociological and political ideas into the mainstream of
educational planning. The work of progressives such
as Susan Isaacs is critically examined.

178 Bantock, G. H. *Freedom and Authority in Education*.
Chicago: Henry Regnery, 1952, 212 pp.

A critique of the trends in education and the
cultural framework within which theories and practices evolved. A caution is expressed related to
progressive education from a conservative viewpoint.

179 Beck, Robert Holmes. "Kilpatrick's Critique of
Montessori's Method and Theory", *Studies in
Philosophy and Education*, Vol. 1, Nos. 4, 5,
1961, 153-162.

A recent re-evaluation of the Kilpatrick criticism of Montessori. This material is helpful in
sensing the militancy of the Kilpatrick stand and
assessing such a stand in terms of current practices.

180 Berkson, I. B. *Education Faces the Future*. New
York: Harper and Brothers Publishers, 1943,
345 pp.

The sub-title of this volume is "An Appraisal of
Contemporary Movements in Education". The major focus is on the transitional state of progressive education in America. A policy statement calling for
a re-ordering of priorities concludes this forward
looking examination. A useful critical commentary
in terms of the state of educational change in the
Pre-World War II period.

181 Bestor, Arthur. *Educational Wastelands: The Retreat
From Learning in Our Public Schools*. Urbana: University of Illinois Press, 1953, 226 pp.

An examination of the purpose of education as viewed through school curricula. The dicotomy between social goals and the development of the intellect in the "new education" as contrasted with early goals of progressive education.

182 Bestor, Arthur. "Progressive Education Vs. Regressive Education", in *The Restoration of Learning*. New York: Alfred A. Knopf, Inc., 1955, 459 pp.

This chapter provides a particularly important discussion since it deals with a definition of progressive education from an alleged conservative point of view. Another important feature is its lengthy analysis of high school curriculum changes and includes criticism of the "Follow-up Study" of such change. The ramifications of changes in curriculum as it affected college admissions are of current interest.

183 Bode, Boyd. "Apprenticeship or Freedom", *The New Republic*, Vol. 63, June, 1930, 61-64.

A dialogue. Dewey's thoughts are most pointed as they reflect his feelings on the state of progressive education in the schools. Bode castigates Dewey followers on their seeming inability to understand Dewey's ideas.

184 Breed, Frederick A. "Good-bye Laissez-Faire in Education", *Elementary School Journal*, Vol. 75, Spring, 1975, 86-93.

Reprint of a 1938 article in the Journal calling for a return to teacher-directed programs rather than student-directed programs. A sense of limits relating to school programming is stressed. Academic discipline is seen as a necessary part of the educational process that can easily be lost in student-dominated programs of instruction.

185 Buckholz, Heinrich. *Fads and Fallacies in Present Day Education*. New York: The Macmillan Company, 1931, 200 pp.

A terse view of the changes in the educational scene wrought by the progressive movement by a National Education Association critic. This is a satirical and biting commentary. The forward by William C. Bagley on the pedagogues of the new education is interesting. A book that can still provoke nervous laughter.

186 Cobb, Ernest. *One Foot on the Ground: A Plea for Common Sense in Education*. New York: G. P.

Putnam's Sons, 1932, 248 pp.

This volume by the cousin of the founder of the Progressive Education Association is an interesting account of one man's criticism and appraisal of the movement. The initial chapter, "What is Progressive Education?" is cogent and raises some timely questions. The material represents a strong minority view of the movement and Association by a member.

187   Counts, George S. "Dare Progressive Education Be Progressive?", *Progressive Education*, Vol. IX, No. 4, April, 1932, 257-263.

A sweeping review and look to the future of the movement. The enormity of elements, the vastness of the tasks undertaken by educators in attempting such a change and the future needs of a rapidly changing society are dealt with in this polemic. The social nature of education is stressed.

188   Counts, George S. *Dare the Schools Build a New Social Order?* New York: The John Day Company, 1932, 56 pp. (Re-published 1969, Arno Press, New York)

A review and criticism of progressive schools. A case is built for the need to look forward to the structuring of a theory of social welfare that can then provide direction for education within and for society. A significant influence in its time.

189   Demashkevich, Michael J. *The Activity School*. New York: Little & Ives, 1926, 150 pp.

This volume, prepared as a doctoral thesis, provides for a critical view of the new tendencies in educational method in Western Europe. The social and political implications of such changes in education are raised with some force. The conflict between a humanistic or liberal education versus one based on realism and manual arts provides a focus of attention. Through examination of the socio-political climates in European countries such polarization can be placed in better prospective. This was one of the few books examining the movement in an adverse fashion.

190   Dewey, John. "How Much Freedom in New Schools?", *The New Republic*, Vol. LXIII, July 9, 1930, 204-206 pp.

A later commentary on the experimental education by Dewey admonishing educators to be actively aware

of change and child study and not to rely on past
successes. An interesting assessment of the implications of current trends in the progressive
movement (1920's). Dewey indicates that a reaction
formation was highly probable if casualness and
slavishness to ideas, rather than a pursuit of
knowledge, was followed.

191 Dewey, John. *The School and Society*. Chicago:
         University of Chicago Press, 1899, 124 pp.

A series of lectures dealing with Dewey's views
on the state of schools in the late 1800's. Dewey
took a critical stand indicating distress with the
status and role of schools within a democracy. Detailed cases of school life are presented. The
training of teachers, especially elementary school
teachers, is decried. An early work expanded in the
later volume, DEMOCRACY AND EDUCATION.

192 Flexner, Abraham. "A Modern School". Occasional
         Publications No. 3, General Education Board,
         1923. Originally in *Review of Reviews*, Vol. 53,
         April, 1916, 465-474.

A critical analysis of traditional education.
Professor Flexner called for the building of a modern system of education. This speech was credited
with influencing the opening of Lincoln School at
Teachers College (1917). A call for integration of
subject matter and the development of broad units
of study as a basis for curriculum design and program planning.

193 Graymar, Thurra. *The School at the Crossroads*.
         New York: Funk and Wagnalls Company, 1937,
         247 pp.

An entertaining and sobering appraisal of the
practices in the public schools (1930's) affecting
the image of the institution for the public at large.
This image is seen as a negative one by the author.
Vignettes of very graphic situations involving
teachers and children help to provide for some insight into the implications and processes involved
in the "new education" as it affected teachers attempting to implement administrative directives and
demands. The final chapters set forth a model for
the "Fifteen Unit Plan" providing an over-all schematic for physical and instructional re-design of
schools, particularly as related to urban settings.

194 Hollins, Th. B. (ed.) *Aims in Education---The
         Philosophic Approach*. Manchester: Manchester

University Press, 1964, 135 pp.

Goals of the educational experience are described and discussed in this lecture series from a British point of view. An interesting analysis of the work of John Dewey and its influence on British progressive educational ideas.

195 Hook, Sidney. "Thirteen Arrows Against Progressive Liberal Education", *The Humanist*, Vol. IV, No. 1, Spring, 1944, 1-10.

A stinging assault on thirteen educationalists (Hutchins, Brandt, Noyes, Meiklejohn, Stringfellow Barr) and their attitudes toward higher education.

196 Kandel, I. L. *American Education in the Twentieth Century*. Cambridge: Harvard University Press, 1957, 247 pp.

The public school movement is examined in terms of the faith of the public at large and the government in education through a widespread democratic form open to all. The American ideal of social mobility through education is examined.

197 Kandel, I. L. "Education and Social Disorder", *Teachers College Record*, Vol. XXXIV, No. 5, 359-367.

A strong and important criticism of the ramifications of the progressive movement in the schools. The author, a spokesman for the long-range view of progressive trends in education and society, calls for greater consideration of both ends and means in education.

198 Kavier, Clarence J. "John Dewey and the New Liberalism: Some Reflections and Response", *History of Education Quarterly*, Vol. 15, No. 4, Winter, 1975, 417-443.

An expansion of Kavier's ideas related to Dewey. Kavier critically discusses Dewey's educational theory and presents possibilities for further study.

199 Kilpatrick, William Heard. *The Montessori Method Examined*. Boston: Houghton, Mifflin Company, 1914, 72 pp.

A short book comparing Montessori and Dewey. The arguments raised are biased and now seem dated. In the ensuing decades this argument was used to destroy the validity of Montessori's ideas within the progressive movement.

200 Kilpatrick, William Heard and William W. Bagley,
Frederick Bonser, James Hosic. "Dangers and
Difficulties of the Project Method and How to
Overcome Them: A Symposium", *Teachers College
Record*, Vol. XXII, No. 4, 1921, 283-321.

A fascinating re-accounting of the progress of
the project method through a symposium format. The
material is important in terms of the development
of an understanding of the method as seen from a
range of viewpoints. The cautions are well-stated
and bear some relevance to open classroom practices.

201 Mallon, Paul R. *The Ease Era: The Juvenile Oli-
grachy and the Educational Trust*. Grand Rapids:
William B. Eerdmans Publishing Company, 1945,
119 pp.

A collection of articles by the author opposed to
progressive educational practices. A fiery commentary by a newspaper writer representing lay opposition
to activities within schools as contrasted to organized learning and structured teaching.

202 Nearing, Scott. *The New Education*. Chicago: Row,
Peterson and Company, 1915. Reprinted: New
York: Arno Press, 1969, 264 pp.

The sub-title, "A Review of Progressive Educational Movements of the Day", describes the volume.
A careful and extensive survey of current (1915)
educational practices and future needs. The author
a professor at the Wharton School, Pennsylvania, was
commissioned by the LADIES HOME JOURNAL to prepare
a series of articles on "Successful Public School
Work in the United States". Through visits to
schools, the author recorded his impressions of the
work being done in the most progressive schools of
the nation. An interesting documentation of the
period.

203 Newlon, Jesse H. *Education for Democracy in Our
Time*. New York: McGraw Hill, 1940, 242 pp.

A critical study of society and the role of
education. The needs of a rapidly changing democracy that can be met through schools, curriculum
and teachers are described. Issues are raised by
changes in the direction of the new curriculum. The
stress on reforms in such critical areas: administration, teaching methods and training and curriculum
are raised in succinct and interesting ways.

204 O'Hara, James. *Limitations of the Educational Theory of John Dewey.* Washington, D. C.: Catholic University of America, 1929, 113 pp.

A critique from a sectarian point of view of the usefulness of Dewey's philosophy in educational planning. The author indicates the parameters of workability and the limitations set by a social orientation.

205 Raby, Sister J. M. "A Critical Study of the New Education", *Educational Research Monographs,* Washington, D. C.: The Catholic University of America, Vol. VII, No. 1, March 1, 1932, 123 pp.

An analysis of the question of the child and society as posed by progressive education. The relationship of the goals of Catholic education and the new education are discussed. Catholic schools using such methods are briefly described. An attempt to place the progressive movement into perspective by a Catholic educator.

206 Rugg, Harold and Ann Shumaker. *The Child-Centered School.* New York: The World Book Company, 1928, 359 pp.

An appraisal of the child-centered school by two educators involved in the movement. Sympathetic criticism is preferred. Descriptive materials are provided related to curriculum and daily programs at several schools. Lincoln, Ojai, Parker, City and Country. Background information on the movement is concisely set forth and comparison of operations between schools is made. Defects in the operations of child-centered schools are noted and discussed particularly in relationship to teachers. A bibliography is included.

207 Salz, Arthur and Mortimer Smith. "A Further Discussion of 'The Truly Open Classroom'", *Phi Delta Kappan,* Vol. 55, No. 9, May, 1974, 627-628.

The argument between Salz and Smith related to the implementation of progressive ideas and techniques in open classroom settings is joined in this summary article.

208 Sandifer, Sister M. R. *American Lay Opinion of the Progressive School.* Washington, D. C.: Catholic University of America Press, 1942, 209 pp.

A study of non-professionals' (men and women), as
revealed in an analysis of magazine articles, views
toward progressive education. The view of the
Church is evidenced in the chapter on progressive
education and its aims. The research design is
slender. The articles used are listed in the bibliography and can be of further interest to readers
involved in research in this area. The summary and
conclusions includes a listing of positive and negative criticism in checklist format. The study is of
interest since it brings together material on the
non-public school attitude toward the changes in
public institutions.

209   Sargent, Porter. *Between Two Wars: The Failure of
      Education, 1920-1940*. Boston: Porter Sargent,
      1945, 608 pp.

      A salty and free-wheeling commentary on the state
      of schools, children, and society during the period
      between World Wars I and II. Written as an anti-
      establishment, anti-western culture statement the
      material reflects a highly personal view.

210   Smith, Mortimer. *And Madly Teach: A Layman Looks
      at Public School Education*. Chicago: Henry
      Regnery Company, 1949, 107 pp.

      A conservative view of the philosophical and
      more practical aspects of the new education. The
      book is directed to the public-at-large. A critique
      of the Teachers College Bulletin on courses avail-
      able is included and quite scathing. This slender
      volume provides a reflection of the then current
      thoughts on the future of the new education. Read
      in the light of the time, the material has interest
      value.

211   Smith, Mortimer. "Before and After 'The Truly Open
      Classroom'", *Phi Delta Kappan*, Vol. 55, No. 6,
      February, 1974, 390-392.

      A critic of the progressive movement addresses
      himself to an article by Dr. Salz calling for a move
      of the traditional curriculum to a more open struc-
      ture. Citing the progressive past as evidence, a
      case is made to evaluate in terms of past success
      and failure.

212   Smith, Mortimer. *The Diminished Mind*. Chicago:
      Henry Regnery Company, 1954, 150 pp.

      The sub-title of this work is A STUDY OF PLANNED
MEDIOCRITY IN OUR PUBLIC SCHOOLS and the position

taken is one highly critical of the outcomes of progressive education. The dominant view (progressive)
of thirty years of educational prominence has resulted in severe consequences for students and
society at large in the author's reflections. It is
argued that disciplined knowledge has been phased
out and replaced with adjustment, mediocrity, and
anti-social service. It is posited that the primary
function of the school should be as transmitter of
the intellectual and cultural heritage of the society and, as part of the process of transmitting, teach
children to think and buttress moral values of the
society. A strong position.

213 Wales, John N. *Schools of Democracy*. Lansing,
       Michigan: Michigan State University Press, 1962,
       161 pp.

       A personal account of impressions and considera-
tions of an English educationist related to secondary education in Michigan. The author is well-
grounded in the ideas of the progressive movement
and attempts to view current practices (late fifties)
in such terms. The study is an interesting one
since it provides the reader with a foreigner's view
of the changes affected by the new education at the
secondary level.

Crosslistings:

       89   Boyd
       117   Hissong
       127   Langford
       129   Maritain
       176   White
       250   Dewey
       404   Bourne

F CURRICULUM

214 American Educational Research Association. *Review of Educational Research*, Vol. VII, No. 2, April, 1937, 199 pp.

An issue devoted to curriculum development, one of the triennial reviews of research conducted by AERA. A number of studies related to the social basis of curriculum are critically evaluated. The extensive experimentation in plans of reorganization of the curriculum related to social experiences is considered. Studies on the Activity Curriculum (experimentation and evaluation) are included. Selected studies on school systems including appraisals of curriculum round out the comprehensive nature of this issue. Authors include: Henry Harap, Hollis Caswell, William Wattenberg, Edith Mitchell, Robert Pooley, William Gray, Paul McKee and Paul Hanna.

215 Andrus, Ruth. *Curriculum Guides for Teachers of Children From Two to Six Years of Age*. New York: Reynal & Hitchcock, 1936, 299 pp.

The curriculum developed through the New York State Department of Education is revealed through the work of teachers and children. Records of actual classroom activities, administrative development of materials are included. A focus on the kindergarten is sharply revealed through photographs, bibliographic materials and equipment lists for activities. An important guide in its time.

216 Association for Supervision and Curriculum Development. *Fostering Mental Health in Our Schools*, *50th Yearbook*. Washington, D. C.: National Education Association, 1950, 320 pp.

A recapitulation of the mental health approach inherent in the progressive programs in many schools. The need for a developmental approach to curriculum design and classroom planning at all levels is substantiated throughout the text. A final section on record-keeping, including observation, anecdotal

records, and sociometric measures as well as the use
of creative experiences to develop better understanding of individual needs is very well done. Many
photographs accompany the text.

217 Bagley, William. *The Educative Process*. New York:
     The Macmillan Company, 1905, 358 pp.

     An early work analyzing the educative process in
     terms of its function, organization and techniques.
     Experimental activity is seen as a required dimen-
     sion. The place of values in development of curri-
     ulum is given prominence in this early attempt to
     refocus the aims of education.

218 Bain, Winifred. *Parents Look at Modern Education*.
     New York: D. Appleton-Century Co., 1935, 330 pp.

     This is a book written for parents rather than
     about them. New programs from nursery through elem-
     entary school are described in detail with attention
     to questions parents might raise. It is informative
     and provides a simple retrospective look at "Modern
     Education" and its practices. A bibliography is in-
     cluded.

219 Baldwin, William A. *From the Old to the New Educa-
     tion*. Boston: New England Publishing Company,
     1930, 191 pp.

     Project work is described and analyzed. The New
     Education as a reaffirmation of the development of
     an independent thinker and doer is posited. The
     role of the teacher is clarified in terms of the
     need for child development and study to facilitated
     guidance of the child in scientific thinking. Use
     of short case studies for illustration. Some chap-
     ter summaries compare old and new methods in terms
     of specific issues and procedures.

220 Barnes, Emily and Bess Young. *Children and Archi-
     tecture*. New York: Bureau of Publications,
     Teachers College, Columbia University, 1932,
     353 pp.

     This study of the work of a sixth grade class at
     the Lincoln School is a thorough recording of the
     project approach. The topic is architecture, a
     sophisticated one. Through co-operative planning,
     trips, activities and research an integrated ap-
     proach to curriculum emerges. The book includes
     day-to-day as well as long-range planning. As a
     curriculum model it is a valuable record of pioneer-
     ing work in unifying curriculum. Contents of the

unit and bibliography are included.

221 Baxter, Tompsie and Bess Young. *Boats and Naviga-*
        tion. New York: Bureau of Publications, Teachers
        College, Columbia University, 1933, 219 pp.

        A lively account of the work of a fifth grade in
        a unified curriculum project related to boats and
        navigation. The materials used and produced by the
        children are described in detail. The integration
        of all areas in a curriculum through a single topic
        is examined and appreciated through this case hist-
        ory approach. An early model of the project method
        in action.

222 Benedict, Agnes. *Dare Our Secondary Schools* Face
        the Atomic Age? New York: Hinds, Hayden &
        Eldredge, 1947, 55 pp.

        A challenge, based on the famed "Eight Year
        Study" of secondary schools, for change. This short
        work supports the need for large-scale change in cur-
        riculum and goal orientation of high school students.

223 Blow, Susan E. *Educational Issues in the Kindergar-*
        ten. New York: D. Appleton and Company, 1908,
        387 pp.

        The effect of the scientific doctrine of relativ-
        ity as it relates to educational planning particular-
        ly in the early years is examined. An historical
        view of influences upon programs is made (Herbart,
        Froebel). New trends in socialization (Kilpatrick)
        are examined by the author. The issues are well
        structured in terms of relevancy of emerging curric-
        ulum.

224 Bobbitt, John Franklin. *The Curriculum.* Boston:
        The Houghton Mifflin Company, 1918, 295 pp.

        The relationship of the application of scientific
        methodology to curriculum design is explained by one
        of the advocates of scientific activity analysis.
        The author is committed to a rational approach to
        curriculum construction involving an analytic survey
        of social behaviors. Stress is laid on development
        of curriculum from such material, providing activi-
        ties and content that reflect a responsiveness to
        society's needs.

225 Bobbitt, John Franklin. *The Curriculum of Modern*
        Education. New York: McGraw Hill Book Company,
        Inc., 1941, 419 pp.

The new education is seen as a dynamic force with a clear theory of curriculum undergirding the structure. "The good life" in its multi-dimensions is seen as both process and goal in the educational process. The text is well-knit and reflects the thinking of an educator involved in curriculum appraisal and development over the first half of the twentieth century.

226 Bonser, F. G. *The Elementary School Curriculum.* New York: The Macmillan Company, 1920, 466 pp.

A careful setting forth of the organization of the elementary school curriculum for the activity program. The difficulties of transition from a subject curriculum to an activity-integrated curriculum are presented. Suggestions related to such transitions are set forth in a detailed manner suitable for all school personnel (classroom teachers, supervisors, administrators). The basic need to have the primary school engaged in purposeful school activities related to life, rather than more abstract subjects, is at the crux of such curriculum change for the author, a professor of education at Teachers College.

227 Bonser, F. G. and Lois Mossman. *Industrial Arts for Elementary Schools.* New York: The Macmillan Company, 1927, 491 pp.

An early work addressing itself to the need to provide for "real life" learning through industrial arts at the elementary school level. The need to have activities which would involve children in both a physical and intellectual participation in school learning is substantiated.

228 Boyd, William, (ed.) *Towards a New Education.* New York: Alfred Knopf, Inc., 1930, 497 pp.

The significant fifth world conference (1929) at Elsinore by the New Education Fellowship has been documented in this volume. The "new" psychology and curriculum possibilities are well described in a series of papers reflecting international trends. This is a most comprehensive presentation of the range of thinking related to progressive education during this period.

229 Burke, Agnes and F. T. Wilson. "Reading Readiness in a Progressive School", *Teachers College Record,* Vol. XXXVIII, April, 1937, 565-580.

A description of an early childhood readiness program to provide for experiences and activities that

foster enthusiasm and interest in beginning reading.
The development of language skills in terms of initial reading needs is clarified. An early documentation of a language arts approach to reading.

230 Burton, William H. *The Guidance of Learning Activi-
     ties*. New York: Appleton-Century-Crofts, Inc.,
     1952, 581 pp.

     The use of the unit plan as a matrix for experi-
     ences and learning based on the needs of children.
     Cooperative pupil-teacher planning, group activities
     and individual initiative are described. Differences
     between adult-directed and child-centered curriculum
     are discussed with a great deal of illustrative back-
     ground information.

231 Carey, Alice, Paul Hanna and J. L. Meriam. *Cata-
     logu of Units of Work, Activities, Projects,
     Themes*. New York: Bureau of Publications,
     Teachers College, Columbia University, 1932,
     290 pp.

     This catalogue includes an annotated list of books,
     pamphlets, periodicals and courses of study related
     to units for kindergarten to eighth grade. While
     a good deal of this material is no longer available,
     the source is a valuable one since it provides a
     view of the availability of materials produced up
     to 1932.

232 Caswell, Hollis and Dook S. Campbell. *Curriculum
     Development*. New York: American Book Company,
     1935, 462 pp.

     A basic text on curriculum design. The project
     method is described with enthusiasm. An evaluation
     of programs in a number of cities: Battle Creek,
     Denver, Philadelphia, Almeda provides interesting
     comparative data.

233 Cavallo, Dom. "From Perfection to Habit: Moral
     Training in the American Kindergarten, 1860-1920",
     History of Education Quarterly, Vol. 16, No. 2,
     Summer, 1976, 147-161.

     The conflict between the Froebelians and the pro-
     gressives in terms of the kindergarten program and
     the curriculum implications inherent in the differing
     views of early childhood education. The principles
     of each side are examined and assessed.

234 *Childhood Education*, Vols. I - IX. Washington,
     D. C.: Association for Childhood Education,

1925-1933,

These combined issues reflect trends in early
childhood education during this active and significant period (1925-1933). A range of articles and
reviews gives an interesting picture of activities
and practices of the time.

235 Clarke, Eric. *Music in Everyday Life*. New York:
W. W. Norton and Company, Inc., 1935, 88 pp.

The need for music education and experience in
the curriculum is strongly stated in this volume.
The place of music in the life of the child and the
adult is given weight through the examples used related to the emotional need for music in development.

236 Clouser, Lucy W. and C. E. Millikan. *Kindergarten
Primary Activities Based on Community Life*. New
York: The Macmillan Company, 1929, 307 pp.

Detailed records of a range of units of work for
early childhood classes: kindergarten, first, second and third graders. Included is a lengthy discussion of the development of criteria for determining objectives and selecting units of work. The use
of the community as a focal point for this age group
is early evidence of the interest in expanding the
world of the young child through school experiences
related to living rather than exposing the young
child to a subject-matter curriculum.

237 Collings, Ellsworth. *An Experiment With a Project
Curriculum*. New York: The Macmillan Company,
1923, 346 pp.

Experimentation with the early "project method"
in a rural setting. The determination of curriculum
based on a wide range of projects: drama, story-
telling, book production, handiwork and trips. The
accounts of activities is interesting and provides
some balance to the work accomplished through this
method in urban settings.

238 Collings, Ellsworth. *Progressive Teaching in Secondary Schools*. Indianapolis: The Bobbs Merrill
Company, 1931, 528 pp.

A view of the possibilities of using newer techniques at the secondary level. The project method
is one of the techniques described in this extensive
review of changes in curriculum design at this level.

239 Cook, H. Caldwell. *The Playway: An Essay in Educational Method*. New York: Frederick Stokes Company, 1915, 366 pp.

An early individual view of the direction which education should take. Written by an English school master, the future activity method is described in great detail (including photographs). Playmaking, or drama as a central activity, is the focus. Reform of the English system is called for and the questions raised by the author, related to the role of education in individual lives, is still current, G. Stanley Hall indicated interest and enthusiasm for this work.

240 Cox, P. W. L. *The Junior High School and Its Curriculum*. New York: Scribners, 1929, 474 pp.

The Junior High school is viewed as a working laboratory in which a great deal of the child's preparation for adult life in a democracy can be accomplished. The possibilities of the new curriculum are described and the basic philosophical structures are clearly presented. The Deweyan idea of trying out a variety of adult possibilities is the model used for this laboratory approach.

241 Crow, Charles. *Creative Education: Some Relations of Education and Civilization*. New York: Prentice-Hall, Inc., 1937, 456 pp.

The integration of education and life through school experiences. Arguments, material and documentation on the value of creative experiences through a creative educational program are presented. A developmental approach is taken to such planning and curriculum. Anecdotal material in support of the material is provided.

242 Culverwell, E. P. *The Montessori Principles and Practices*. London: G. Bell & Sons, Ltd., 1914, 309 pp.

Montessori education as a progressive move from the traditional British approach to education is proferred to teachers and parents. Historical antecedents to the philosophy and methodology are discussed. Careful descriptions of apparatus. The use of such materials with children in classes is covered.

243 Curtis, Neil A. *Boats*. Chicago: Rand McNally & Co., 1927, 145 pp.

This work, based on the author's experiences at
the Lincoln School, Teachers College, New York, reflects the day-to-day activities of the class as
they developed a unit of work on boats. Using the
children's interest, a scheme for enriching the
language arts areas of the curriculum is illustrated.
Books appropriate for use with children and teachers
are included. Kilpatrick wrote the introduction.

244 Dalcroze, Emile Jacques. *Rhythm, Music, and Education.* New York: G. P. Putnam's Sons, 1921,
334 pp.

The philosophy and instructional designs of Dalcroze. An active approach to the learning and teaching of music to children from early childhood through
the teens. This basic work was widely used in progressive circles.

245 Dewey, Alice C. "The Place of the Kindergarten",
The Elementary School Teacher, January, 1903,
273-288.

The significance of kindergarten as a transitional
experience between home and school for the young
child is stressed. The positive role kindergarten
can effect is highlighted. Child study and curriculum development are carefully related throughout. A
very useful article for those interested in the relatedness of early childhood to the new education.

246 Dewey, John. *The Child and the Curriculum.* Chicago:
University of Chicago Press, 1902, 40 pp.

The child study developmental approach to curriculum design is detailed. A need to focus on the
child as the center for all curriculum standards is
the major thesis postulated with force. The relationship between thinking and subject-matter teaching
is analyzed.

247 Dewey, John. "Froebel's Educational Principles",
Elementary School Record, No. 1, February,
1900, 143-151.

Dewey attempts to utilize key elements of Froe-
belian theory related to the child as an educational
resource. Spontaneous activity in the guise of games,
play and peer interactions are discussed as foundational sources for use in schools. An interesting
article since it places the early kindergarten practices within the context of the emerging "new education".

248   Dewey, John. *Progressive Education and the Science of Education*. Washington, D. C.: Progressive Education, Vol. V, July-September, 1928, 197-204.

An important address made at the eighth annual conference of the Progressive Education Association. The role of teachers and administrators in providing guidance related to individual needs, specifically intellectual needs in the development of curriculum and programs of study in progressive school programs.

249   Dewey, John. "The University Elementary School, Studies and Methods", *University (of Chicago) Record*, May 21, 1897, complete issue.

Dewey reports to parents and staff on the state of the Laboratory School. He clarifies initial aims and elaborates on current practices in some detail. An important article as it states, in simple language, how curriculum practices related to children's needs developed at the Laboratory School under the tutelage of Professor Dewey.

250   Dewey, John and Evelyn Dewey. *Schools of Tomorrow*. New York: E. P. Dutton and Company, 1915, 316 pp.

This highly significant volume is the result of collaborative reflections (Dewey and his daughter) based on Evelyn's visitations to a number of progressive schools. The outcomes, both academic and vocational, of such training are examined in terms of a democratic order. The requirements of teaching related to a society's future needs are detailed through an examination of past and present trends as observed in schools. The focus is set on thinking as a process that should be given exercise in schools. The ramifications of adapting curriculum to the abilities of children, as well as their interests, are central to this study. The programs and philosophy of the schools visited are documented with enthusiasm and sensitivity. This book became a popular work having a wide audience in the decade following publication.

251   Dewey, John and James McLellan. *The Psychology of Number and Its Application to Methods of Teaching Arithmetic*. New York: Appleton-Century-Crofts, Inc., 1895, 309 pp.

An early work melding the newer psychology (functionalism) and pedagogy (scientific) and setting guidelines for the teaching of arithmetic functions

in classrooms. The material is dated but the attempt
to define classroom practices along more scientific
lines is of interest.

252 Dill, Nancy. "An Inquiry into Curriculum Theories
     and Open Classroom Practices", *Notre Dame Journal
     of Education*, Vol. 3, No. 2, Summer, 1972, 140-
     150.

     The progressive movement is one of the areas ex-
     amined in terms of the curriculum possibilities in
     the open classroom movement.

253 Eakright, Jessie B. and Bess Young. *Adventuring
     With Toys*. New York: Bureau of Publications,
     Teachers College, Columbia University, 1933,
     242 pp.

     A two year case study of the development of a unit
     of study for fourth grade children engaged in an
     aesthetic experience with toys. Clear presentation
     providing a vivid picture of decision making, group
     work and individual interests. The arts are seen as
     educative forces in the curriculum. An interesting
     bibliography related to toys is provided.

254 Elementary Curriculum Series, Territory of Hawaii.
     Activity Program for the Primary Grades. Terri-
     tory of Hawaii: Department of Public Instruction,
     1930, 105 pp.

     The Department of Public Instruction provided
     this curriculum guide to help teachers better under-
     stand both the rationale and implementation of activ-
     ity programs. The statement of purpose is clear.
     The plans are most interesting in terms of their
     current value, e.g. discussing doll centered activ-
     ities: "Boys are more interested if there are some
     boy dolls supplied." Year by year activities are
     included through grade three.

255 Elementary Teachers and Supervisors of the State of
     Utah. *Educative Elements in the Environment of
     the School Child of Utah*. Salt Lake City: De-
     partment of Instruction, 1937, 57 pp.

     A curriculum guide based on the unit plan of study
     and directed toward the use of the natural environ-
     ment in the elementary school. Thoughtful utiliza-
     tion of Utah's natural resources for school study
     provide an ecological and environmental package of
     interest.

256 Featherstone, W. B. "The Speyer School for Slow-
     Reading Children", *Teachers College Record*,
     Vol. 38, February, 1937, 365-380.

     A comprehensive picture of this unusual experi-
     ment in public education wherein children with read-
     ing difficulties were grouped (five classes of low
     normal IQ 75-90) into two classes of gifted children
     in a single school. The activity program was used
     to help facilitate work in basic skill learning.

257 Forest, Ilse. *The School for the Children From
     Two to Eight*. Boston: Ginn and Company, 1935,
     286 pp.

     This volume represents the author's course mater-
     ial for "Kindergarten-Primary Education" from the
     summer sessions at Connecticut State Teachers' Col-
     lege held at Yale University. These seminars were
     very much a part of the progressive education move-
     ment to provide in-service experiences for retrain-
     ing and refinement of teacher skills. The material
     is useful for both supervisors and teachers. The
     organization is simple, curriculum practices and
     procedures, planning, housing and integration of ex-
     periences are included. Special attention is given
     to reading instruction, record-keeping and testing.
     Bibliographic material appears after each chapter.

258 Fowler, B. P. *Educative Enterprises in School and
     Classroom*. Wilmington: The Tower Hill School
     Association, 1925, 37 pp.

     A modest bulletin that presents the work initiated
     by pupils in this progressive school. The work re-
     veals activities in a number of curriculum areas and
     reflects the schools's philosophy of student initia-
     tion of projects and group activities.

259 The Francis W. Parker School, Chicago: Yearbooks
     (approximately 150 pp. each):
     Vol. I   *The Social Motive in School Work*, 1912
     Vol. II   *The Morning Exercise as a Socializing
               Influence*, 1913
     Vol. III *Expression as a Means of Training
               Motive*, 1914
     Vol. IV   *Education Through Concrete Experience*,
               1915
     Vol. V   *The Course in Science*, 1918
     Vol. VI   *The Individual and the Curriculum:* Ex-
               periments in Adaptation, 1920
     Vol. VII *Social Science Series: The Course in
               History*, 1923

Vol. VIII *Creative Report,* 1925

A series of eight volumes reflecting the work at the Francis S. Parker School in Chicago. These works present a picture of the curriculum from primary through high school. The books are of importance both singly and as a body since the theoretical, as well as the practical, applications of the work conducted at the school are carefully presented and appear within a context of an active school. Since the work conducted at this school became a standard for much that was to come in the "new education", the material is of particular interest in this original state.

260 Harmer, Althea. "Elementary Cooking in the Laboratory School", *The Elementary School Teacher,* Vol. III, No. 10, 1903, 706-709.

Cooking as a medium for practice in scientific methodology appropriate to the curiosity and interests of primary school children is carefully described. Age-related findings and group techniques are presented. An important paper with valid material for today's teachers.

261 Hartman, Gertrude. *The Child and His School.* New York: E. P. Dutton and Company, 1922, 248 pp.

A work commissioned by the Bureau of Educational Experiments to provide a resource for teachers engaged in the development of new programs and activities. The author starts at a foundational level and builds a framework of understanding of the child. The educational possibilities are then described in great detail. Each chapter includes readings for the teachers and Part III of this volume provides an extensive bibliographic resource for the development of units of study on selected topics.

262 Hartman, Gertrude and Ann Schumaker (ed.) *Creative Expression.* New York: The John Day Company, 1939, 2nd ed., 350 pp.

An important text providing a range of articles related to the arts and creative expression in curriculum planning. Creative expression through music, art, literature and dramatics originally published as four special issues of Progressive Education (1926, 1927, 1928, 1931).

263 Hildreth, Gertrude. *Learning the Three R's.* Minneapolis: Educational Publishers, Inc., 1936, 824 pp.

A basic text on the beginning of basic skill learning. Readiness in terms of the best progressive principles of child development is given ample space. The beginning techniques of reading, writing, and number work are accorded extensive coverage. This text was an important resource in teacher training courses related to the primary grades,

264 Hill, Patty (ed.) *A Conduct Curriculum for the Kindergarten and First Grade*. New York: Scribner, 1924, 123 pp.

The development of the conduct curriculum is detailed. An analytic study of current (circa 1920) trends and needs related to formulation of objectives, appropriateness of activities, and anticipated outcomes for kindergartners and first graders as reflected in the newer curriculum. An important book in its time having a wide audience among teachers and administrators in both early childhood and primary education programs.

265 Hollingshead, Arthur D. *Guidance in Democratic Living*. New York: Appleton-Century, Inc., 1941, 260 pp.

A report of teachers and principals of the Ashland School, East Orange, New Jersey, over a nine year period. The development and implementation of a high school program of socialization. Learning situations, teaching situations, and guidance procedures are carefully set forth. A summary chapter provides interesting evaluative material.

266 Hosic, James and Sara Chase. *Brief Guide to the Project Method*. Yonkers: World Book Company, 1924, 243 pp.

A compact text establishing a positive view of the Project Method. Illustrations of the method in action includes clarification of the role of teacher, problems in implementation and specific project reports. Photographs are included.

267 Hughes, Avah Willyn. *Carrying the Mail*. New York: Bureau of Publications, Teachers College, Columbia University, 1933, 253 pp.

A second grade's social studies program built around the mail becomes the core for a year's work as described in this volume. Illustrations of children's work, unit plans for a range of subject areas related to the postal system (e.g. communication, transportation, etc.) are included.

268   Irwin, Elizabeth and Louis A. Marks. *Fitting the
       School to the Child: An Experiment in Public
       Education.* New York: The Macmillan Company,
       1924, 339 pp.

       A descriptive study of the movement carried out
       in a large (3000 children) New York City public
       school (P.S. 64) from 1916 to 1922. Grading proced-
       ures were used to help determine the kinds of educa-
       tional experiences individual children needed. This
       school gave rise to the Little Red Schoolhouse as a
       result of its being turned into a junior high school
       and the relocation of its teachers and students to
       another physical plant. The program described is an
       ungraded one. Mainstreaming of students is suggested
       and developed. As an historical reference point, this
       volume is of value because of the germinative nature
       of the ideas and practices and as a contrast to cur-
       rent operations of the Little Red Schoolhouse.

269   Johnson, Marietta. *Youth in a World of Men.* New
       York: The John Day Company, 1929, 325 pp.

       A child-study and development view of the need
       for change in the education of children. Activities
       are described and plans for curriculum expansion and
       enrichment are presented.

270   Jones, Thomas Jesse. *Four Essentials of Education.*
       New York: Charles Scribner's Sons, 1926, 188 pp.

       The needs of communities, particularly those that
       are rural, are addressed in this volume. The reflec-
       tion of such needs in the development of school pro-
       grams and curricula is substantiated through a strong
       defense related to the future of children served in
       rural settings.

271   Keelor, Katherine Louise. *Indian Life and the Dutch
       Colonial Settlement.* New York: Bureau of Pub-
       lications, Teachers College, Columbia University,
       1931, 314 pp.

       A source book and text for the study of early
       colonial life. Units of work for third grade stu-
       dents are included. These units were developed
       during the 1929-30 school year at the Lincoln School,
       New York, and represent examples of curriculum exper-
       imentation within a child development framework. In-
       dividual growth charts of children are included.

272   Keelor, Katherine Louise. *Working With Electricity.*
       New York: The Macmillan Company, 1929, 109 pp.

A unit of work on the role of electricity in everyday life. This volume, developed for use with primary grade children, is a resource for experiments
and integrated work in science.

273   Keelor, Katherine Louise. *Curriculum Studies in the
      Second Grade*. New York: Bureau of Publications,
      Teachers College, Columbia University, 1925,
      130 pp.

      Work at the Lincoln School, New York, in the de-
      velopment of a second grade curriculum based on
      child development principles and reflecting the needs
      of children is described in detail. A unit involving
      the creation of a play city is finely drawn. Re-
      sources and suggested activities are included. The
      goals of group work and social understanding are
      clarified.

274   Kilpatrick, William Heard. "The Project Method",
      Teachers College Record, Vol. XIX, No. 4, 1918,
      319-335.

      A seminal article on the project method of the
      soon-to-come activity program. This article was a
      rallying cry for a new means of organizing learning.
      The traditional role of curriculum areas as being
      discrete parts of the educational plan was attacked
      and a new integrated sense of curriculum definition
      is postulated.

275   Klapper, Paul. *The Teaching of History*. D. Apple-
      ton and Company, 1926, 347 pp.

      A study of problems related to the teaching of
      history and current events in elementary through
      junior high schools. The impact of the new educa-
      tional demands is experienced throughout the text.
      Projects, values clarification, courses of study
      and testing are dealt with at length. A substantive
      work that was influential in its time.

276   Krackowizer, Alice M. *Projects in the Primary Grades*.
      Philadelphia: J. P. Lippincott Company, 1919,
      221 pp.

      The value of the Project Method as a means of
      studying the child, providing for social experiences
      and developing skills (reading, writing and numbers)
      is raised. The material is based on experiences in
      elementary schools, particularly kindergarten and
      first grade. The function of integration of experi-
      ences and subject matter through group projects is a
      central theme. Photos are provided throughout the

text. An early and influential work.

277 Lane, Robert H. *A Teacher's Guide Book to the Activ-
     ity Program*. New York: The Macmillan Company,
     1932, 257 pp.

     A compact text which included a schematic of im-
plementation possibilities for the activity program.
Units of work by theme, daily programs schedules and
teaching practices culled from the work of over two
dozen teachers helps to reveal classroom practices
embedded within the progressive-activity approach.
Assessment material is included.

278 Lee, Joseph. *Play in Education*. New York: Mac-
     millan Company, 1919, 500 pp.

     A plea for the use of physical activity within
the school day. An early call for the extension of
the curriculum to include the whole child (physically
and intellectually) in the process of education.

279 Maguire, Edward R. *The Group Study Plan*. New York:
     Charles Scribner's Sons, 1928, 203 pp.

     The innovative technique of the Group Plan, a
method of teaching through pupil participation, is
carefully described in this volume. The author is
committed to such change and provides material to
support the view that pupil's learning through participation has a stronger and more lasting effect
than teachers teaching to the class. A persuasive
documentation of this position.

280 Mearns, Hughes. *Creative Power*. New York: Double-
     day, Doran and Company, 1929, 396 pp.

     A record of the findings of the author's experi-
ments in teaching related to the new trend of developing creative faculties. A description of classroom
work at the Lincoln School in New York is given. Particular emphasis is placed on prose and verse. This
volume offers an interesting contrast to some of the
work in the English public schools centered around
poetry, prose and drama. Creative writing, as a
substantive area of language arts, was given impetus
through this popular work.

281 Mearns, Hughes. *Creative Youth*. Garden City:
     Doubleday, Doran and Company, 1925, 234 pp.

     A companion volume to CREATIVE POWER written five
years earlier. This volume expresses the child development point of view in terms of the developing
child's need to express himself in a variety of art

forms: music, art, language and drama. The need
for activity within programs is verified through
lively examples.

282 Melvin, A. Gordon. *Method for New Schools*. New
     York: The John Day Company, 1941, 301 pp.

     The need for "wholeness", for integration of
     experience, living and ideas is part of the basic
     thrust of this work. Curriculum areas are described
     in great detail with specific attention to develop-
     ment within an area and closure possibilities. Broad
     school curricula needs and opportunities are set
     forth. The idea of "incidental learning" as it re-
     lates to the 3 R's is presented in interesting per-
     spective. The text became a required book for those
     engaged in the activity program.

283 Meriam, Junius. "An Activity Curriculum in a School
     of Mexican Children", *Journal of Experimental
     Education*, Vol. 1, No. 4, June, 1933, 308-366.

     A description of the activity program implemented
     in a school with non-English speaking children. Aca-
     demic skills are developed and assessed. The program
     includes language learning through plays, stories
     and handiwork. The activity element is seen as the
     key to learning skills.

284 Meriam, Junius. *Child Life and the Curriculum*. New
     York: World Book Company, 1920, 338 pp.

     A basic text on the construction of curriculum
     based on child study and development principles.
     The author was a key figure at the University of
     Missouri Elementary School and the material is an
     accounting of the experimentation and practices at
     the school. The activity curriculum is examined in
     terms of the (then) current problems necessitating
     change in the traditional subject matter of schools.

285 Miller, Harry L. and Richard T. Hargreaves. *The
     Self-directed School*. New York: Charles Scrib-
     ner's Sons, 1925, 412 pp.

     The authors, principals in high school, attempt
     to deal with ways in which creative thinking can be
     developed through school experiences. The focus is
     on the development of self-active, socially respons-
     ible citizens of a democracy particularly at the high
     school level. The need for guidance and semi-curri-
     cular activities is established. Useful material on
     the role of adolescents within the school setting.

286 Milwaukee Public School. *Projects and Games in the*
     Primary Grades. Milwaukee: The Milwaukee Board
     of School Directors, 1921, 173 pp.

     A collaborative effort by teachers and administra-
     tors of projects and activities appropriate for pri-
     mary grade use. Part I provides a "synopsis of the
     project method" that is clear and useful. Part II
     is the "plan for project teaching in first grade".
     This section includes material on particular projects
     in some detail. Games are clearly described, photos
     are included. The relevance to contemporary ap-
     proaches is apparent.

287 Minor, Ruby. *Early Childhood: Its Principles and*
     Practices. New York: D. Appleton-Century Com-
     pany, 1937, 763 pp.

     The role of the kindergarten and primary grades
     in the educational process is exhaustively described.
     The progressive nature of the development of early
     childhood educational programs is stressed as a major
     factor in their acceptance for the "new education".
     An emphasis on the educative process and the early
     years. A definitive work of sizable proportions.
     Very detailed bibliographic material appears at the
     end of each chapter. Part III, "organization of ex-
     perience with reference to a clarification of subject
     matter", provides for half the content. The position
     established through this work is that of centrist for
     the progressive movement.

288 Minor, Ruby. *Pupil Activities in the Elementary*
     Grades. Philadelphia: Lippincott, 1929, 260 pp.

     A presentation of the "unit" concept of organiz-
     ing the curriculum. Detailed projects for the elem-
     entary school grades are included. Specific project
     aims and the means to obtain such goals with a pro-
     ject-centered curriculum are provided. Written at
     the mid-point of the popularity of the project method,
     this book had considerable appeal in the decade that
     followed and provides interesting material for com-
     parison with Open Classroom curriculum organization.

289 Montessori, Maria. *The Montessori Elementary Mater-*
     ial. New York: Frederick A. Stokes Company, 1917,
     464 pp. (Translated by Arthur Livingston) Re-
     published by Robert Bentley, Inc., 1964.

     Part Two of the original Montessori, THE ADVANCED
     MONTESSORI METHOD, this volume provides detailed ma-
     terial on the content and practices involved in the
     teaching and learning of grammar, reading, arithmetic,

geometry, drawing, metrics and music. A basic Montessori text.

290 Montessori, Maria. *The Montessori Method*. New York: Frederick A. Stokes Company, 1912, 377 pp. (Translated by Anne E. George) Republished by Schocken Paperback, 1964; introduction by J. McVicker Hunt.

The original work on the scientific pedagogy related to the education of the child from three through six years of age. Extensive material on early development, the Montessori apparatus and the relatedness of developmental process, e.g. the senses to early learning of basic skills. This work was later refined by the Doctor and appeared as THE DISCOVERY OF THE CHILD.

291 Montessori, Maria. *Spontaneous Activity in Education*. New York: Frederick A. Stokes Company, 1917, 384 pp. (Translated by Florence Simmonds) Republished by Robert Bentley, Inc., 1964.

Volume One of the ADVANCED MONTESSORI METHOD, covering the education of children from seven through eleven. Developmental material on the child is covered: will, imagination, attention, intelligence. The role of the teacher in preparing children for learning and content for children are described. A basic foundational work of Montessori.

292 McMurray, Charles. *Excursions and Lessons in Home Geography*. New York: The Macmillan Company, 1920, 152 pp.

An early work on the uses of field trips for geography learning. Trips to local scenic areas, shops, factories, gardens, farms, dairies and government buildings are described. Generalized material related to such trips is included and interesting.

293 McMurray, Charles. *Special Method in Geography*. New York: The Macmillan Company, 1905, 217 pp.

A course of study for third through eighth grade. Both methodology and curriculum content is presented in detail. The use of home excursions and observations is described. A neglected area can be viewed through this text.

294 McMurray, Charles. *Teaching by Projects: A Basis for Purposeful Study*. New York: The Macmillan Company, 1920, 257 pp.

The Project Method is described in detail. Levels
of projects: large units, object lessons, classroom
methods based on projects are developed. An interesting contribution which provides basic information
related to this educational innovation.

295   National College of Education. *Curriculum Records of
       Children's School.* Evanston, Illinois: Bureau
       of Publications, National College of Education,
       1932, 562 pp.

       A basic text on the activity program. Units are
       developed for all levels and by grade (kindergarten
       through sixth). Model lessons and units are pro-
       vided. An interesting aspect of this book is the
       description of typical school days at different
       grade levels. Record-keeping materials are de-
       scribed.

296   National Society for the Study of Education. *The
       Foundations and Technique of Curriculum Construc-
       tion.* Twenty-sixth Yearbook. Bloomington, Illin-
       ois: Public School Publishing Company, 1927.
       Two volumes.

       A classic two volume work marking the maturity of
       curriculum design as requirement in educational plan-
       ning. These volumes, the outcome of the National
       Society's committee on curriculum making, reflect the
       child study focus and support of the new movement in
       education. The need for social development through
       school experiences emerges as a strong element in
       curriculum design. A diverse and important reflec-
       tion of the range of ideas related to the function
       of curriculum by the leaders of the twenties: Rugg,
       Counts, Charters, Bonser, Kilpatrick, Kelly, Bagley,
       etc. An inventory and critique of past and present
       practices is included. A triad of trouble composed
       of problems involved in integration of Dewey's ideas
       on democratic education, the need for social effic-
       ency and the data of child study is suggestive.

297   New York City Board of Education. *Extended School
       Services Through the All Day Neighborhood Schools.*
       New York: Board of Education Curriculum Bulletin
       No. 3, 1947, 86 pp.

       A review of the program to extend school service
       in the schools. The needs of children and committees
       in the delivery of such service is detailed. An at-
       tempt to bring activity program possibilities to a
       larger number of school children in an urban setting.

298 Noar, Gertrude. *Freedom to Live and Learn.* Philadelphia: Franklin Publishing and Supply Company,
1948, 159 pp.

Problems of curriculum reconstruction related to
the junior high school are clarified in this volume.
The unit approach is the focus. Techniques are presented for selecting and developing appropriate units
of learning. A practical presentation with day-to-
day records of unit progress. One of the few books
dealing with the newly formed level of the junior
high school.

299 O'Shea, M. V. (ed.) *The Child: His Nature and Needs.*
New York: The Children's Foundation, 1924, 516 pp.

A sizable survey supervised by O'Shea, a professor
of education at the University of Wisconsin, reflecting the breadth of understanding related to the developing child and his needs. Programs of education
and material on educational trends are cited in pro-
fusion. Material on preventing delinquency and on
adolescents is well detailed.

300 O'Shea, M. V. *Newer Ways with Children.* New York:
Greenberg Publishers, 1929, 419 pp.

The child-study movement provides material for
the development of techniques of meeting specific
needs of children in home settings. Contrast of
older methods of adult-child relationships with
newer ones reflecting the progressive trend is provided.

301 Parker, Francis. *How to Study Geography.* New York:
D. Appleton and Company, 1894, 405 pp.

This notable text on geography was written by
Francis Parker in 1889. Geography was seen as a
critical subject area allowing for integration of
subject matter (history, math, reading, science).
Graded material is offered giving some range to the
content.

302 Patty, William L. *A Study of Mechanism in Education.*
New York: Teachers College, Columbia University,
1938, 183 pp.

A study from a relativistic point of view of
mechanistic approaches to the work of Bobbitt, W. W.
Charters and C. C. Peters. This volume reflects the
critical examination of ideas related to both curriculum and educational psychology that was part of the
progressive era.

303 Prescott, Daniel A. *Emotion and the Educative Process*. Washington, D. C.: American Council on Education, 1938, 323 pp.

This important work, commissioned by the Council on Education in response to a need to define the nature of the education of adolescents in a changing world order, was an important book having some impact on the consideration of changes at the secondary level. A re-reading, despite the passage of years, can be of value to those interested in secondary education. The focus on the emotional life of the adolescent as a necessary factor in the design of programs is significant.

304 Reed, Mary and Lula Wright. *The Beginnings of the Social Sciences*. New York: Charles Scribner's Sons, 1932, 224 pp.

The early school years in kindergarten and first grade are revealed as the foundational years in social science learnings. Through well developed chapters, the authors present the content, organization and functioning of such a curriculum. Illustrations are included as well as anecdotal material on the experiences of young children. An interesting introduction by Patty Smith Hill is provided to this work.

305 Rugg, Harold, et al. *Democracy and the Curriculum: The Life and Program of the American School*. New York: D. Appleton-Century Company, 1939, 536 pp.

A study of "The American Problem" for teachers, youth and parents. This study, based on the efforts of a group of educationists including Kilpatrick, Hanna, Counts and Zachry, details the work of the Progressive Education Association as it related to curriculum development. A final section on "The Life and Program of the Schools" points to future needs and possibilities. In the light of history this section is of particular surprise and interest.

306 Salisbury, Ethel. *An Activity Curriculum*. San Francisco: Harr Wagner, 1924, 142 pp.

A small volume bringing the need for an activity curriculum to the fore through a statement of its value in motivating children to perfect skills (reading, writing, mathematical). Classroom activities are described and explained in terms of motivation.

307 Slavson, S. R. *Creative Group Education*. New York:
     Association Press, 1937, 247 pp.

     A book on process in group leadership and teaching
as it related to integration of the whole child within an educational context. The relationship of the
group to individual personality development forms a
basis for curriculum development and expansion. The
club program, field trips, creative arts and special
summer group programs are discussed in terms of both
theoretical and practical aspects. A career line of
educational consultant is presented. The appendix
includes a record of an activity club over a period
of time and records the progress of a therapy group.
Written by one of the leaders of the group therapy
movement, this volume provides educators with one
view of the newer possibilities inherent within a
progressive education framework that has been given
little attention in research.

308 Smith, Nila Blanton. *American Reading Instruction*.
     New York: Silver Burdett Company, 1934, 287 pp.

     A state of the art volume describing the practices
and techniques used in comtemporary (progressive and
traditional) settings. A very good resource in terms
of changes in reading instruction during this period.

309 Spears, Harold. *The Emerging High School Curriculum
     and Its Direction*. New York: The American Book
     Company, 1940, 400 pp.

     A most comprehensive view (text and photographs)
of high schools engaged in experimentation and
change. The problems are dealt with in depth and
the practices described in a manner that enlightens
as well as informs.

310 Stevens, Marion P. *The Activities Curriculum in the
     Primary Grades*. Boston: D. C. Heath & Company,
     1931, 440 pp.

     A practical guide for teachers of children from
kindergarten through fourth grade. The material is
organized so that units of work are made available
as they relate to formal skills. The author was a
teacher at the Ethical Culture School in New York.
Curriculum plans, materials and equipment required
to implement such plans and guidelines for progress
are included. The implications of program design on
the social needs of children are stressed. A related bibliography is included.

311   Stiles, Dan (pseud.) *High Schools for Tomorrow.*
      New York: Harper Brothers, 1946, 212 pp.

      A personal statement that is very provocative.
      The author attempts to convey the crucial need for
      change at the secondary level in terms of rapidly
      changing social and economic conditions. He stresses
      a child development approach to this age group as
      well. The goals of a good secondary education are
      defined.

312   Stolper, J. R. and H. O. Fenn. *Integration at Work:*
      Six Greek Cities. New York: Bureau of Publica-
      tions, Teachers College, Columbia University,
      1939, 166 pp.

      Utilizing Greek citizens and cities as models of
      democratic functioning, a group of high school stu-
      dents engaged in a ten-week project which is described
      in this volume. The project was designed to promote
      integration of experiences and knowledge. The study
      guide is very complete and could be used to advantage
      by teachers in planning such a project of theme poss-
      ibilities for their classes today.

313   Stoddard, George D. and Beth C. Wellman. *Child*
      Psychology. New York: The Macmillan Company,
      1934, 419 pp.

      Child development is examined in terms of current
      research on the nature of the child. This volume
      was considered an important resource in the develop-
      ment of curriculum during the thirties. Research
      methodology is explained. Special behavior, play and
      creativity are probed through related research find-
      ings.

314   Storm, Grace E. *Social Studies in the Primary Grades.*
      New York: Lyons and Carnahan, 1932, 596 pp.

      A basic text on the activity program. The setting
      up of classroom activity units that involve the child
      in social, industrial and domestic learnings as well
      as reinforcing and teaching basic skills related to
      the social studies.

315   Stull, DeForest. *Tentative Course of Study in Geo-*
      graphy. New York: Bureau of Publications,
      Teachers College, Columbia University, 1927,
      288 pp.

      A cooperative effort by teachers at the Horace
      Mann School, New York City, and the author, a pro-
      fessor at Teachers College. Extensive material for

primary, intermediate and junior high is included. Units of work are described, some anecdotal material and related bibliography are also included. The style is a narrative one and the material is organized by school levels which is helpful. Test questions are provided giving some indication of the goals expected of teachers and children.

316 Thayer, V. T., Caroline Zachry and Ruth Kotinsky. *Reorganizing Secondary Education.* New York: Appleton-Century-Crofts, Inc., 1939, 483 pp.

This sizable contribution was commissioned by the Progressive Education Association (1932) in the hopes of calling attention to the need for massive change within secondary schools. The curriculum at this level had resisted change during the twenties and thirties and dire sounds were heard related to re-evaluation of the academic goals. The study was extensive and the authors represented both the mental health and pedagogical sides of the issue. A book worth current examination.

317 Thomas, William and Dorothy Swaine. *The Child in America: Behavior Problems and Program.* New York: Alfred Knopf, Inc., 1928, 321 pp.

A comprehensive view of the state of child welfare in the United States. Several chapters reflect on the changing schools and the newer programs designed to help meet special needs of children.

318 Tippett, James S. et al. *Curriculum Making in an Elementary School.* Boston: Ginn & Company, 1927, 359 pp.

This volume, produced by the staff of the famed Lincoln School, provides material on curriculum making in an experiemntal setting. Criteria for decision making related to courses of study, description of work units and resource possibilities are provided. Extensive descriptive material on several units is included.

319 Tippett, James S. *Schools for a Growing Democracy.* Boston: Ginn & Company, 1936, 338 pp.

An account of an experiment in unit instruction through the democratic process at the Parker School District (circa 1927). This was an eight year experiment that is clearly presented to advantage for administrators and teachers interested in the relationship between school staff and children.

320 Waddell. C. W., Corrinne Seeds and Natalie White.
     Major Units in the Social Studies. New York:
     The John Day Company, 1932, 389 pp.

     A useful volume describing the integrated program
     in an activity school. The program centered around
     social studies with extended activities in the arts
     and physical education. Units of work are provided
     for the fourth, fifth and sixth grades.

321 Ward, Florence E. *The Montessori Method and the
     American School.* New York: The Macmillan Com-
     pany, 1913, 243 pp.

     The author, a professor of education at Iowa State
     College, provides material related to the apparatus
     and material of a Montessori program. She discusses
     their application to comtemporary American problems
     (1910). Individual activity, as opposed to collective
     class exercises, freedom of movement and responsibil-
     ity for work by the student are described and given
     credence as valid educational goals. The implica-
     tions for better adjustment of pupils to school work
     through application of this method are postulated.
     An early integration of the movement to liberalize
     the school program.

322 Wells, Margaret. *The Project Curriculum, How the
     Present Came from the Past.* Philadelphia: J.
     B. Lippincott Company, 1921, 338 pp.

     A definitive work on the use of the project as
     a matrix for curriculum development. Major projects
     for the early primary grades are explicitly detailed.
     An experiment in the Trenton (New Jersey) schools is
     documented.

323 Whipple, Guy M. (ed.) *The Activity Movement, Part II,
     The Thirty-third Yearbook of the National Society
     for the Study of Education.* Bloomington: Public
     School Publishing Company, 1934, 320 pp.

     This yearbook of the NSSE focuses on the activity
     movement and curriculum changes. The controversial
     nature of the issues involved is considered in de-
     tail. The varieties of practices termed "activity"
     are examined and an attempt is made to present a
     balanced view. Statements by individual members of
     the committee are made available and provide inter-
     esting material for current consideration. A se-
     lected bibliography is included.

324 Whipple, Guy M. (ed.) *Child Development and the
     Curriculum, Part I, The Thirty-eighth Yearbook*

of the National Society for the Study of Education.
Bloomington: Public School Publishing Company,
1939, 448 pp.

The relatedness of child development to curriculum
design and implementation is given coverage in this
yearbook. The design and fit of instructional materials and activities to the developmental level of
the child in order to meet educational objectives
was a significant concern among progressive educators. The articles include an introduction by Carleton Washburn and cover traditional and newer curriculum areas, e.g. "Radio and Motion Pictures" by
Arthur Jersild. A final section on appraisal and
needed research points to both the complexity of
such integration and suggests ways of studying
change. An interesting volume to consider in light
of current trends toward the open education plan.

325 Woodring, Maxie N. and R. T. Benson. *Enriched*
       Teaching of English in the High School. New
       York: Teachers College, Columbia University,
       1927, 104 pp.

An early resource for high school English teachers
of enrichment materials. The materials cited include
sources for free materials on debating, dramatics,
books. The material is of interest in that it reveals the depth and range of the enrichment possibilities in an activity-directed secondary program in
English.

326 Wright, Lula E. *A First Grade at Work.* New York:
       Bureau of Publications, Teachers College, Colum-
       bia University, 1932, 247 pp.

The activity program developed for a first grade
class involved in preparation for reading rather
than grade one reading. An interesting argument for
preparatory experiences extending over a long period
(one year) at the first grade level. This is a highly suggestive volume in terms of current trends in
early reading instruction and problems related to
the increase in non-readers at the upper grades.

327 Zachry, Caroline. "The Influence of Psychoanalysis
       on Education", *Psychoanalytic Quarterly*, Vol. 10,
       1941, 431-444.

The effects of psychiatric interest on the outcomes
of the educational process are considered in terms of
needed input in curriculum design and educational
planning. Particular attention to newer methods of
education and ramifications of integration of mental

health attitudes is provided.

328 Zirbes, Laura. *Curriculum Trends*. Washington,
     D. C.: Association for Childhood Education,
     1935, 39 pp.

     This interesting forecast of future curriculum
trends, based on a review of literature on the pre-
ceeding period, described in some detail a variety
of the newer programs. The trends described can be
examined in terms of educational developments of the
forties and fifties to advantage.

Crosslistings:

52	Bagley	384	Plummer
64	Dewey	385	Progressive Educa-
68	Froebel		tion Association
78	Washburne	392	Tyler
79	Bagley	394	Wilson
94	Cobb	395	Wrightstone
100	Dewey	396	Zirbes
113	Hamaide	400	Biber
118-119	Isaacs	401	Blackburn
134	McGregor	402	Blatz
139	Rainwater	403	Bourne
144	Stevenson	406	Clapp
146	Washburne	407	Clouser
148	Wilson	408	Corlett
153	Cusden	410-411-412	DeLima
154	Fediaevsky	413	Dewey (E.)
156	Ferriere	414	Dewey (J.)
157	Grant	415	Dix
182	Bestor	417	Garrison
200	Kilpatrick	418	Goodlander
203	Newlon	419	Hartman
206	Rugg	420	Henley
331	Crawford	421	Horrall
332	Forest	422	Isaacs
333	Gray	423-424	Johnson
335	Heffron	425	Lewis
343	Lambert	426	Lynch
344	Lane	427	Mayhew
346	Melvin	428	MacConnell
348-349	Montessori	429	McMurray
350-351	Mossman	430	Parkhurst
354	Porter	433-434-435	Pratt
356	Sloman	437	Slight
359	Strickland	440	Stott
360	Aiken	441	Washburne
372-373	Gates	445	Wofford
383	New York State	448-449	Burr
	University	458-459	McKown

329   Bagley, William and J. T. Alexander. *The Teacher of The Social Studies*. New York: Charles Scribner's Sons, 1937, 328 pp.

A sizable text on the methods and rationale of social studies teaching. Particular emphasis on the role of values clarification through this subject area. The increased responsibility of teachers within this subject area for the social development of children is shown.

330   Burton, William. *The Nature and Direction of Learning*. New York: D. Appleton-Century Company, 1929, 595 pp.

A teacher-training volume concerned with the thinking of Herbart and the new experimental psychologists (Judd, Thorndyke). Learning theory for teacher activities related to specific goals and procedures are methodically described. Material related to the new education and the project method is analyzed. A substantive teaching manual.

331   Crawford, C. C. and L. P. McDonald. *Modern Methods of Teaching Geography*. New York: Houghton Mifflin, 1929, 306 pp.

This book was written for teachers and in-training teachers. Historical trends in the teaching of geography reveal shifts in emphasis over the years. Practical aspects related to implementation through a variety of means: lab activities, projects, readings, games and visual aids are provided. The material is extensive.

332   Forest, Ilse. *The School for the Child from Two to Eight*. Boston: Ginn and Company, 1935, 286 pp.

A classic text on early childhood practices and programming. An outgrowth of the famed summer sessions given by the author at Connecticut State Teacher's College held annually at Yale University. Record keeping and testing material is of interest.

333 Gray, William. "Implications for Teacher-Training
of the New Educational Plan at the University of
Chicago", *Teachers College Journal*, Vol. III,
No. 1, September, 1931, 50-59.

A review of the radical reform of curriculum at
the University of Chicago as it effected teacher-
training. Curriculum which would offer "breadth of
training" involving the teacher-to-be in the major
fields of learning, allowing for advanced study in
specific fields and facilitating research. An early
argument for a broader form of training.

334 Heaton, K. L., W. C. Camp and P. B. Dietrich. *Professional Education for Experienced Teachers*.
Chicago: University of Chicago Press, 1940,
142 pp.

The role of in-service training in the re-educa-
tion of teachers for the newer curriculum and program
possibilities is explained. A description of the
summer workshop movement to serve such an end is helpful. The summer workshop movement enjoyed popularity
during the thirties when wide-spread teacher re-educa-
tion was needed.

335 Heffron, Ida C. *Francis Wayland Parker: An Inter-
pretive Biography*. Los Angeles: Ivan Deach, Jr.,
1934, 127 pp.

A personalized biography of Colonel Parker written
by an art teacher in the Chicago and Cook County Normal School. The work of Parker as a leader of the
new movement in teacher training and educational
practices is viewed in terms of his own growth and
development. The relationship between Dewey and
Parker is clarified. The progression of Parker-in-
spired schools: Ojai Valley, Shady Hill, Francis W.
Parker, North-Shore-Winnetka, San Diego and Hessian
Hills is described and historical continuity documented up to the Winnetka experiments of Washburne.

336 James, William. *Talks to Teachers on Psychology*.
New York: H. Holt and Company, 1939 edition,
238 pp.

This classic work by James was given a new introduction written jointly by Dewey and Kilpatrick in
this edition. They indicate the validity of James'
material in terms of the newer ideas and practices
in education. Suggestions are made for teachers to
attend to James as they pursue change in their classrooms.

337 Judd, Charles H. "The Training of Teachers for a
     Progressive Educational Program", *Elementary
     School Journal*, Vol. 75, Spring, 1975, 78-85.

     A reprint of an article first published in the
     Journal in April of 1938. Professor Judd defends
     the traditional in the face of progressive changes
     in the schools.

338 Kandel, I. L. *The Cult of Uncertainty*. New York:
     The Macmillan Company, 1943, 129 pp.

     The fifteenth volume of the Kappa Delta Pi Lec-
     tures deals with the presentation of issues involved
     in "the cult of change". An argument is put forth
     for a return to reason in education and teacher
     training. The problems generated by conflict within
     the culture are described and the effects of educa-
     tion are discussed. The timing (1943) provides a
     perspective on both the direction and ramifications
     of pragmatic (progressive) theories and practices.

339 Keliher, Alice V. *Life and Growth*. New York:
     Appleton-Century-Croft, Inc., 1938, 245 pp.

     An activist in child study and development pre-
     pared this volume in response to a need to help
     clarify the questions asked by students in training
     related to technique and practices in the newer
     schools. Based on information obtained through
     questions asked by students, the material has an
     active quality.

340 Kelley, Earl C. *The Workshop Way of Learning*.
     New York: Harper and Brothers, 1951, 169 pp.

     Experiences at Wayne University in the Education
     Workshop (started in 1938 by Dean Lessenger and Dr.
     J. Emens) are detailed. This year-long, one evening
     (4:30-9:00 p.m.) per week format, open to undergrad-
     uates and graduates, was seen as an innovative tech-
     nique in training teachers with the newer methods.
     Student teachers and experienced teachers were in-
     volved in these credit-bearing workshops. An ex-
     cellent resource document for those involved in cur-
     rent teacher resource centers. Evaluation materials
     are involved.

341 Kilpatrick, William Heard. *Foundations of Method:
     Informal Talks on Teaching*. New York: The Mac-
     millan Company, 1925, 383 pp.

     Methodology as the nexus of teaching is developed
     in this series of lectures. This is an elementary

approach to learning theory. Through the use of the Socratic dialogue, the author attempts to answer educational questions formulated by students. The book has a loose quality to it that tends not to substantiate its argument as a foundational work of methodology.

342 Kilpatrick, William Heard (ed.) *John Dewey Society First Yearbook: The Teacher and Society*. New York: Appleton-Century Company, 1937, 360 pp.

A collection of provocative essays related to teachers, their training and the supervision provided in schools. The administrative problems in the newer schools are described as a reflection of the increased size of schools and the increased problems of management.

343 Lambert, Clara. *From the Records: An Adventure in Teacher Training*. New York: Child Study Association of America, 1939, 138 pp.

Summer play schools offered teacher trainees in the late thirties an unusual opportunity for reorientation to the newer progressive methods for use in their classrooms. This book describes the project with care and a great deal of insight. The final chapter includes age-group diaries (5-6, 7-8, 9-10) that provided interesting material for current comparison.

344 Lane, Robert H. *The Teacher in the Modern Elementary School*. New York: Houghton Mifflin Company, 1941, 397 pp.

Educational practices for the classroom teacher in a progressive school are described. This is a text designed to provide scientific guidelines related to classroom management. Practices of everyday curriculum implementation are indicated for use by teachers. An updating of material in the earlier (1932) volume, A TEACHERS GUIDE BOOK TO THE ACTIVITY PROGRAM.

345 Melvin, A. Gordon. *Progressive Teaching*. New York: D. Appleton and Company, 1929, 272 pp.

Rubrics for a scientific foundation of teaching are set forth. The philosophy and psychology involved in teacher training which will meld into a theory of activity in teaching is described. The text includes discussion on the historical development of education, child development, questions related to readiness for learning, intelligence, testing and the effect of environment on learning.

346 Melvin, A. Gordon. *The Technique of Progressive Teaching*. New York: The John Day Company, 1932, 405 pp.

This book is directed to teachers and to student teachers. It provides pedagogical material on basic learning theories, fundamentals of technique, classroom arrangement, directed learning and teaching patterns as experiences in the newer "progressive" schools. Units of work are provided and a bibliography is provided that closely relates to the content of the units. A book that received wide attention in its time and set a pedagogical framework for use in many normal school training programs.

347 Monroe, Walter. *Teacher-Learning Theory and Teacher Education, 1890-1950*. Urbana: University of Illinois Press, 1952, 426 pp.

An historical study of the developments in teacher education and teaching-learning theory. A sizable accounting that helps to clarify some of the divergent thinking and educational practices of the progressive movement. An important resource.

348 Montessori, Maria. *The Discovery of the Child*. Madras, India: Kalakshetra Publications, 1948, 398 pp. (Translated by Mary A. Johnstone).

The definitive Montessori text. This edition was the final revision, substantially enlarged, of THE MONTESSORI METHOD. The translator, Mary A. Johnstone, an art historian and writer, has rendered the English version in excellent style. She worked directly with Madame Montessori on this translation (which could not find a publisher in England during war time and was finally published in India). Other translations are available. The material is far more comprehensive than the original and shows the development of both text and ideas over the years. All areas of the curriculum in a Montessori setting are carefully detailed and the developmental data to support such practices are provided.

349 Montessori, Maria. *Dr. Montessori's Own Handbook*. New York: Frederick A. Stokes, 1914, 189 pp.

A handbook designed for teachers explaining the basic Montessori approach to education. This volume is dedicated to Helen Keller and Anne Sullivan. Dr. Montessori notes that Miss Keller personifies the possibility of education of the senses and Miss Sullivan personifies the ability of the teacher to learn from her pupil. The material is less refined than that to be found in DISCOVERY OF THE CHILD.

350 Mossman, Lois C. *Principles of Teaching in the Elementary School*. New York: Houghton Mifflin, 1929, 292 pp.

A guide for teachers to the use of newer procedures in the classroom. Relationship of current practices to knowledge of learning is presented. Curriculum and general teaching methods are detailed. An emphasis is given to the social matrix of learning.

351 Mossman, Lois C. *Teaching and Learning in the Elementary School*. Boston: Houghton Mifflin Company, 1929, 292 pp.

The newer programs of instruction developed through the activity program are described. The basic principles undergirding such programs of interactive learning are explained. Methods of implementing such principles through practice are extensively discussed. The author prepares a set of criteria for evaluation of learning and instruction through such techniques.

352 Palmer, A. R. *Progressive Practices in Directing Learning*. New York: Macmillan Company, 1929, 300 pp.

A practical guide for the classroom teacher in planning and structuring learning using newer methodologies. Materials on individualization of learning based on diagnosis of specific difficulties is provided. Development of teaching aids toward individual learning needs.

353 Parker, Samuel C. *General Methods of Teaching in Elementary Schools Including Kindergarten*. Boston: Ginn and Company, 1919, 336 pp.

An interesting text on methodology focusing on newer educational purposes. Written as a text for teachers in training by a professor of educational methods at the University of Chicago, the material reveals insights into social and individual needs. The final chapter on "Differences in Capacity" presents a significant view of the more progressive educationists of the time.

354 Porter, Martha P. *The Teacher in the New School*. New York: World Book Company, 1930, 312 pp.

A personal account of the way in which a progressive teacher worked. The major portion of this volume covers the author's work as a teacher of eight year old children in the third grade as the Lincoln School, New York City. This vivid account of class-

work provides material that supports the theoretical
position of curriculum based on children's interests.
The text provides criteria for selection of units,
describes in detail techniques used in starting activities developing study habits and in relating intellectual interests to skills and creative work.
The results of a year's work is evaluated. The function of activity in the child's development is clarified. Of particular interest is the material on ways
of adapting such a method for classroom use. A bibliography is included.

355 Rugg, Harold. *The Teacher of Teachers*. New York;
     Harper and Brothers Publishing, 1952, 308 pp.

     This volume on teacher-training is the result of
thirty years' experience and reflection on the subject by the author. The period from 1925-1950 is
singled out as a significant one in terms of new
theoretical and practical aspects in teacher education. The author has prepared a case against a
liberal arts education and proposes a new university
discipline in education. The influence of the progressive movement is evident and the creative direction in training is stressed. An annotated bibliography for teachers is included.

356 Sloman, Laura Gillmore. *Some Primary Methods*. New
     York: The Macmillan Company, 1927, 293 pp.

     An introductory text for younger teachers on the
newer methods in primary education (progressive,
activity, project). The project method is investi-
gated in detail. Examples of projects are examined,
e.g. a film of "Peter Rabbit" made by a second grade
class seems remarkably current. The role of seat-
work in classrooms is explained. Activities are
suggested to help make such work lively and meaning-
ful to children. Reading, language and arithmetic
are presented as substantive areas for projects and
activities. Photos accompany this thoughtful text.

357 Smith, Eugene Randolph. *Some Challenges to Teachers*.
     New York: Exposition Press, 1963, 191 pp.

     A series of thoughts directed towards teachers
and students preparing to teach. The author, founder
of the Park School in Baltimore (1912) and the Beaver
Country Day School in Massachusetts (1921), was a
pioneer in mathematics education. His progressive
views emerge in these short, crisp chapters, addressed to ideas, means and feelings in teaching.

358   Smith, Nila Blanton. *Adventure in Teacher Education*.
      San Jose, California: Steward Publishing Company,
      1937, 200 pp.

          The results of four years' experimenting at the
      Broadoaks School of Education at Whittier College
      with the new educational practices and philosophy.
      The work of student teachers is of particular in-
      terest.

359   Strickland, Ruth G, *How to Build a Unit of Work*.
      Washington, D. C.:   Federal Security Agency,
      U. S. Office of Education, 1946, 48 pp.

          This handbook was developed to help teachers in
      a wide range of settings become more familiar with
      unit-centered classroom practices.   It is carefully
      drawn and descriptive units are developed to illus-
      trate the process.

Crosslistings:

      113   Hamaide
      154   Dottrens
      164   Makarenko
      203   Newlon
      257   Forest
      263   Hildreth
      289-290-291   Montessori
      314   Storm
      452   Gustin

H   EVALUATION AND RECORD-KEEPING

360   Aiken, Wilfred M. *The Story of the Eight Year Study*.
New York: Harper & Brothers, 1942, 157 pp.

An accounting of the results of an experiment with
the activity program and progressive education at the
high school level. Thirty high schools participated
in the study. Through curriculum modification students were released from the college entrance requirements that were standard end goals in these high
schools. An assessment of student interests, provi-
sion of innovative curriculum and ongoing evaluation
procedures help to provide guidelines for future experimentation in curriculum change at the high school
level. A standardization of methods for setting objectives was obtained through this assessment process.
A follow-up study was conducted by Ralph Tyler as the
students became college students.

361   Andrus, Ruth. *A Tentative Inventory of Habits of
Children from Two to Four Years of Age*. New
York: Bureau of Publications, Teachers College,
Columbia University, October 11, 1924, 50 pp.

An interesting and useful model developed to record the behavior and activities of the young child.
The intention of this work was to help provide classroom teachers and nursery workers with objective criteria for assessing such behaviors. The material
gathered could then be used for development of activities based on child study data. Later revised (1928)
and issued as: AN INVENTORY OF THE HABITS OF CHILD-
REN FROM TWO TO FIVE YEARS OF AGE.

362   Blos, Peter. *Trait Studies in a Progressive School*.
New Orleans, Metairie Park Country Day School,
1936, 42 pp.

An analysis of the material collected in the Metairie Country Day Schools, New Orleans, related to
the developmental needs of children and the school
program. An interesting finding indicates that even
in the best schools (those with a progressive program)

little use was made of the child's home life and the
involvement of parents in the educational process.

363 Bruechner, Leo J. et al. *The Changing Elementary
     School*. New York: Inor Publishing Company, 1939,
     388 pp.

The New York State Regents conducted a large scale
inquiry in 1935 into education. Part of the inquiry
was a study of the elementary schools. This report
of the findings is of particular interest since it
recommended changes related to both administration
and curriculum. Since schools in the cities, particularly in New York, had engaged in the activity
program, the study merits attention.

364 Brusse, Bun Bates and F. C. Ayer. *An Activity Pro-
     gram in Action*. Dallas: Banks, Upshaw and Com-
     pany, 1935, 197 pp.

A report on the implementation of the activity
program in Houston, Texas. Focusing on a year of
an upper fourth, lower fifth grade, teacher planning,
implementation, and evaluation are discussed. A
chapter on individual pupil adjustment and social
progress is a particularly useful one. The final
chapter on outcomes provides material from children
and parents.

365 Chamberlin, Charles Dean et al. *Did They Succeed
     in College?: The Follow-up Study of the Thirty
     Schools*. New York: Harper & Brothers, 1942,
     291 pp.

Report of the Commission on the Relation of School
and College of the Progressive Education Association.
This study of the graduates of the "thirty schools",
in which experimental curriculum was made available,
when they entered college is a valuable one. Criteria were established and evaluations made on some 3600
students. Differences between graduates from the selected progressive high schools and traditional high
schools were minimal. Similarities in scholastic ap-
titude, social and economic backgrounds were seen as
common levelers. Intangible items, e.g. resourceful-
ness, were seen as important. Criteria and instru-
ments used are described in the appendix.

366 Class of 1938, University High School. *Were We
     Guinea Pigs?* New York: Henry Holt, 1938, 303 pp.

A startling book written by former students in a
progressive high school. A critical look backwards
of the six-year secondary school lives of students.

The core program, the curriculum, the attitude of
teachers and students are examined from two per-
spectives: the students' and retrospectively in
terms of present experiences. A rare volume.

367 Cohen, Ronald D. *The Gary Schools and Progressive
      Education in the 1920's.* Washington, D. C.:
      American Research Association, 1975, 32 pp.

A re-evaluation and review of the Gary Schools
during the progressive era of change. An interesting
aspect of this review is the inclusion of material on
differences between black and white students in the
Gary Schools.

368 Collings, Ellsworth. "A Conduct Scale for the Meas-
      urement of Teaching", *Journal of Educational
      Method*, November, 1926, 97-103.

Record-keeping for the classroom teacher is illustrated through the development of a scale for meas-
uring children's responses related to interests,
motivation and activities, A corollary use for the
development of teaching difficulties based on a
separate inventory for teacher use is described. A
useful approach to child study techniques as they apply to classroom mamagement.

369 Cowell, C. C. "Diary Analysis: A Suggested Tech-
      nique for the Study of Children's Activities and
      Interests", *Research Quarterly.* May, 1937, 15-18.

An interesting account of an approach to data collection from observation and interactions with children. The illustrations used are clear and the method
is described as it relates to enriching work with
children in classrooms.

370 Flexner, Abraham and Frank Bachman. *The Gary Schools:
      A General Account.* New York: General Education
      Board, 1918, 265 pp.

An analysis of Gary, Indiana, and its educational
needs and assets. The Gary Plan of moving toward a
progressive system in theory, structures and practice is described with considerable detail. This is
a summary volume of the findings (which included
ocven volumes) of the evaluation of the "Gary Plan"
affecting the total school system. The evaluation
was financed by the Rockefeller sponsored General
Education Board. It is a cautious and careful assessment of this innovative and trend-setting experiment.
The plan was a massive one involving the creation of
an entire city's public education system and its in-

fluence was international.

371   Forest, Ilse. *Pre-school Education*. New York:
      The Macmillan Company, 1929, 413 pp.

      This historical and critical study of the early
      childhood movement provides a review of pre-school
      trends. The impact of contemporary ideas and the
      new education on current trends (1920's) is high-
      lighted by a description of programs and related
      studies of historical interest. An evaluation of
      programs includes those of day nurseries, kinder-
      gartens, and nurseries with shortened days is based
      on material developed from the Merril Palmer School
      and the Yale Guidance Clinic.

372   Gates, Arthur and Guy Bond. "Some Outcomes of In-
      struction in the Speyer Experimental School (P.
      S. 500, New York City)", *Teachers College Record*,
      Vol. 38, December, 1936, 206-217.

      A report on the work of the first six grades at
      the Speyer Experimental School (under the auspices
      of the Board of Education, New York City and Teach-
      ers College). Five of the classes were classified as
      dull normal (I.Q. 75-90). This school, with an
      activity enriched program provided students with a
      remedial educational experience that reflects pro-
      gress through the findings of the study. The stu-
      dents were the subjects of extensive testing.

373   Gates, Arthur. "Systematic vs Opportunistic Teach-
      ing", *Teachers College Record*, Vol. 23, April
      1926, 679-700.

      A review of research conducted to determine the
      effectiveness of systematic subject matter instruc-
      tion and opportunistic teaching based on children's
      interests and activities. The experiment is care-
      fully detailed and the findings are provocative.

374   Greene, Katherine. "Activity Education", *Review of
      Educational Research*, Vol. XII, No. 3, June, 1942,
      280-288.

      Report of research on activity education covering
      the period of the thirties. The New York City Public
      School's experiment is reviewed. Experimentation on
      the secondary and college levels is included. Sources
      for procedures in evaluation are suggested particular-
      ly as they relate to assessment of learning within an
      active structure of instruction.

375 Gunther, Theresa C. *Manipulative Participation in the Study of Elementary Industrial Arts.* New York: Bureau of Publications, Teachers College, Columbia University, 1931, 58 pp.

The interest in experience motivated learning versus text learning was carried over to the testing and assessment of such methods. This study presents the findings of research related to an experimental research project involving the children's learning of facts through texts and first-hand experience.

376 Hall, Mary Ross. *Children Can See Life Whole.* New York: Association Press, 1940, 157 pp.

A study of some progressive schools in action is the sub-title of this work. The material is interesting in that it is an accounting of visitations to a dozen schools and the observations of individual programs are described. There is limited material on direct observation or interviewing with children, however, and the title is more of an inference than a deduction based on material from the children.

377 Hopkins, L. T. and James Mandenhall. *Achievement at the Lincoln School: A Study of Academic Test Results in an Experimental School.* New York: Teachers College, Columbia University, 1934, 64 pp.

An important study reporting on the testing procedures and results over a twelve year period at the famed Lincoln School, Teacher's College, New York. Selected areas of curriculum are examined.

378 Kandel, I. L. *Examinations and Their Substitutes in the United States.* New York: Carnegie Foundation for the Advancement of Teaching, 1936, 183 pp.

The role of examinations in the setting of educational policy is viewed and assessed. A description of the use of examinations in determining programs of instruction, and objectives pursued by teachers and students, raises some fundamental questions.

379 Loftus, John. "New York City Large Scale Experimentation with an Activity Program", *Progressive Education*, Vol. 17, No. 2, February, 1940, 116-124.

A review of the activity program during the thirties in New York City. The material is of interest and details program variations and student performance on tests.

380   Marot, Mary. *Records*. New York: Bureau of Educational Experiments, 1922, 47 pp.

A detailed account of the system of record-keeping at the City and Country School, New York. This small pamphlet helps in understanding the nature of the child study technique of developmental record-keeping in the planning of curriculum and activities within schools.

381   Moore, Annie et al. "Children's Records", *The Classroom Teacher*, Vol. III, 1927, 28-73.

An interesting and unusual description on records that children can construct related to their schoolwork. This material can be helpful to those involved in open classrooms.

382   MacLatchy, Josephine H. "Activity Programs in Nursery School, Kindergarten and Elementary Schools", *Review of Educational Research*. Vol. VII, No. 5, December, 1937, 526-544.

A review of the research on the activity program. A very clear presentation of definitions related to activity education is made. Katherine McLaughlin and Louis Raths collaborated on parts of this interesting review which includes an appraisal of techniques used in determining outcomes of the activity program. The section on social behavior helps to clarify some of the key work in this area. Research on play in relation to development and learning is considered. This is an important article since it reviews a wide range of pertinent studies.

383   New York State University. *The Activity Program.* Albany: State Department of Education, 1941, 182 pp.

A report of a survey on progressive curriculum implementation in the New York City schools. The activity program is examined under the direction of J. Cayce Morrison and contrasted with the more traditional program in most of the schools of the city. The survey design is excellent and this report merits careful reading by those involved in educational decision making. Areas included are: parental attitudes, teacher responses, evaluation of children's work. Particularly interesting is one of the findings related to increased critical reading ability of children in the activity program.

384   Plummer, Gordon S. "Unclaimed Legacy: The Eight Year Study", *Art Education*, Vol. 22, No. 5, May, 1969, 4-6.

The use of the Eight Year Study findings in terms
of core curriculum and the articulation of the arts
to the curriculum at the high school level is es-
posed by the author.

385 Progressive Education Association. *Thirty Schools
     Tell Their Stories*. New York: Harper & Brothers,
     1943, 362 pp.

Thirty secondary schools representing a wide range
of national locales contribute their stories to the
final volume of a five volume series, THE EIGHT YEAR
STUDY (1933-1941) conducted by the Progressive Education Association on high school and college needs.
Some of the schools do not have progressive curriculum. However, the cumulative portrait that emerges
represents a valuable contribution to the understanding of progressive methods and trends as it relates
to high schools and the implications in terms of college requirements and practices.

386 Robinson, Virginia P. "Records as an Aid to Under-
     standing Children", *Progressive Education*, Vol.
     IV, No. 1, October, 1926, 318-322.

A useful set of guidelines detailing the type of
record-keeping that can be accomplished in homes and
schools related to child growth and development. The
material is thoroughly discussed in terms of utiliz-
ation. A bibliography supporting the child-study
approach is included.

387 Rusk, Robert. *An Outline of Experimental Education*.
     New York: St. Martin's Press, Inc., 1960, 118 pp.

An interesting contribution to the field of educational psychology. The author uses material from educational studies of the progressive movement as illustrations. The experimental nature and possibilities of education and the thrust of the change
towards experimentalism are clarified in this work.
The view offered adds to a retrospective understanding of the impact of progressive ideas on education.

388 Ryan, W. Carson. *Mental Health Through Education*.
     New York: The Commonwealth Fund, 1938, 315 pp.

An evaluation of the state of mental health in
schools made by the author after a two year period
(1935-1936) in schools and clinics. This report reflects the impact of the change in schools towards
the new education. It attempts to describe the
changes taking place and to correlate the material
with findings in mental health. Teacher training,

curriculum, administration, parents and community
are included, as well as the child, as significant
dimensions of the educational process. An excellent
reading.

389 Smith, Eugene Randolph. "School Methods of Study-
     ing Children", *Progressive Education*, Vol. III,
     No. 1, 14-18.

     A short, thorough article on record-keeping. In
this case the records suggested are personality pro-
files. Sample worksheets are provided and material
is discussed related to the construction and use of
such material.

390 Stormzand, Martin. *Progressive Methods of Teaching.*
     Boston: Houghton Mifflin Company, 1927, 325 pp.

     Experimentation in the field of teaching technique
related to newer methods and practices is analyzed.
Descriptive and critical analysis of textbook teaching, project methods, laboratory methods, drill and
individualized instruction is covered. The text was
written for teachers engaged in a re-evaluation of
traditional methods and for new teachers interested
in the newer progressive possibilities.

391 Thorndike, Robert et al. "Observations of the Be-
     havior of Children in Activity and Control Schools",
     Journal of Experimental Education, Vol. 10, Decem-
     ber, 1941, 38-45.

     Indicates that children in activity programs are
superior in behavioral skills involving "leadership,
self-initiated enterprises and experimentation". A
small but interesting study.

392 Tyler, Ralph W. (ed.) "Curriculum Development in
     the Twenties and Thirties", *The Curriculum:
     Retrospect and Prospect, Seventieth Yearbook,*
     National Society for the Study of Education,
     Part I. Chicago: The Chicago University Press,
     1971, 364 pp.

     An analysis of the twenty-sixth yearbook of the
NSSE on Curriculum (1927). As a retrospective it
provides useful benchmarks and connectives related
to current trends in curriculum development. The
planning of the Eight Year Study of High Schools is
detailed and a review of the content of the study
is included. A useful companion piece to the Eight
Year Study.

393 Washburne, Carleton W., Mabel Bogel and William S.
     Gray. *Results of Practical Experiments in Fit-
     ting Schools to Individuals: A Survey of the
     Winnetka Public Schools.* Bloomington: Public
     School Publishing Company, 1926, 135 pp.

     The results of a survey of the Winnetka Technique
     on individualization of education (instruction and
     progress) are presented in a concise manner. De-
     tailed material on the technique, the school popula-
     tion, costs, academic achievement, and specific
     controlled experiments, i.e. arithmetic, spelling.
     The findings provide interesting data related to
     individualization of instruction as contrasted with
     class-group instruction.

394 Wilson, Frank and Agnes Burke. "Reading Readiness
     in a Progressive School", *Teachers College Record*,
     Vol. 38, 1937, 565-580.

     A study of the program in reading readiness and
     reading programs operative in the kindergarten and
     primary grades of the Horace Mann School beginning
     1933-1934 and followed through 1937. The kinder-
     garten program is described in detail. Findings
     indicate a serious consideration of such procedures
     in planning for reading skill learning. A detailed
     list of criteria used by the kindergarten teacher
     to assess her judgments on probable reading progress
     of individual children is included.

395 Wrightstone, J. W. *Appraisal of Newer Elementary
     School Practices.* New York: Bureau of Publi-
     cations, Teachers College, Columbia University,
     1938, 221 pp.

     This study included a survey and analysis of
     trends in experimental and conventional schools and
     a comparison of data derived from both groups. The
     material was developed to help provide decision-
     making answers to the comparative efficiency of
     old and new methods. An introductory chapter pro-
     vides a status report of programs in various parts
     of the United States. Curriculum content, practices,
     student adjustment and objectives are included in
     this study. The weight of evidence collected tends
     to favor the newer approaches. This study had a
     great deal of influence on the New York City Public
     School administration.

396 Zirbes, Laura. *Comparative Study of Current Prac-
     tices in Reading, With Techniques for the Improve-
     ment of Teaching.* New York: Bureau of Publica-

tions, Teachers College, Columbia University, 1928, 229 pp.

A significant study dealing with a comprehensive view of reading within the progressive school. Purposes, objectives and activities related to reading instruction are detailed and evaluations are presented.

397   Zyve, Claire. "A Suggestion for Evaluating School Activities", *Teacher's College Record*, Vol. 38, No. 8, May, 1937, 648-659.

One of the more interesting assessment articles related to the progressive education activity program.

Crosslistings:

      2   Alberty
    152   Ash
    216   Association for Supervision and
            Curriculum Development
    232   Caswell
    265   Hollingshead
    295   National College of Teachers
    315   Stull
    318   Tippett
    332   Forest
    351   Mossman
    354   Porter
    403   Bourne
    415   Clapp
    420   Henley
    423-424 Johnson
    429   McMurray
    430   Parkhurst
    433-434-435 Pratt
    439-440 Stott
    444   Winsor
    457   McCall
    462   Public Administration Service
    469   Baldwin

I EXPERIMENTAL SCHOOLS

398 Badley, John H. *A Schoolmaster's Testament*. Oxford:
     B. H. Blackwell, 1937, 209 pp.

     A series of talks given by the headmaster of Bed-
     ales reflecting his forty years of educational ex-
     periences. The intimacy and directness of the mat-
     erial is particularly refreshing. The changes in
     this experimental school over a period of time are
     revealed in the talks.

399 Badley, John H. *Bedales, A Pioneer School*. London:
     Metheun & Co., Ltd., 1923, 231 pp.

     A history of the famed Bedales progressive school
     in England. This school provided a model for many
     others in terms of the curriculum provided and the
     integration of boys and girls in a co-educational
     setting.

400 Biber, Barbara, Lois Murphy, Louise Woodcock, Irma
     Black. *Child Life in School: A Study of a
     Seven Year Old Group*. New York: E. P. Dutton
     & Company, 1942, 658 pp.

     A study of a group of seven year olds at the
     Little Red Schoolhouse in New York. Stages of devel-
     opment, the relationship of curriculum to emerging
     developmental needs and the effects of environment
     were studied. A chapter on the Rorschack test by
     Anna Hartock and Ernest Schactel provides important
     material. This study is a classic of the period as
     it deals with child study and curriculum within a
     specific group over a one year period. The instru-
     ments used are described in detail. Republished
     (1952) as LIFE AND WAYS OF THE SEVEN TO EIGHT YEAR
     OLD. New York: Basic Books, 1952, 658 pp.

401 Blackburn, Mary. *Montessori Experiments in a Large
     Infants School*. New York: E. P. Dutton and
     Company, 1920, 143 pp.

     An extension of Montessori in a large British

infant school is described in detail by the headmistress of the Leeds Demonstration School for City Training College. The author records her experiments with the method in a large urban school in three areas: classification and grouping of children, use of Montessori apparatus and the teaching of reading, writing and numbers. The experiments are carefully described. Both vertical and parallel family grouping of children are presented in detail.

402 Blatz, William E. and Dorothy Millichamp. *Nursery Education: Theory and Practice*. New York: William Morrow and Company, 1935, 357 pp.

The St. George's School for Child Study at the University of Toronto, Toronto, Canada, established in 1926 is the setting for this extensive Canadian work on nursery education. Nursery education is seen as progressive education since its basis is centered in child study and socialization within this setting. Daily programs are included; detailed studies related to routines (sleeping, eating, toileting) are informative. Work and play habits are examined as viable curriculum areas.

403 Bourne, Randolphe. *The Gary Schools*. Cambridge: The M.I.T. Press, 1970, 323 pp. (Reprint of 1916 edition with an introduction and annotations by Adeline and Murray Levine).

The system is described in detail from a positive viewpoint. Curriculum methods and organization of this innovative learning community are placed within a philosophical and sociological framework. An account of large-scale institutional change. Uses of schools by all members of the community and the use of community resources by the schools. The introductory material and annotations are written by a sociologist. An epilogue contains an abridged and annotated version of Flexner and Bachman's summary volume assessment of the system with an introduction by Adeline and Murray Levine.

404 Bourne, Randolphe. "Schools in Gary", "Communities for Children", "Really Public Schools", "Apprentices to the Schools", "The Natural School". Five articles in the *New Republic*, March 27, April 3, April 10, April 24, May 1, 1915.

Impressionistic, very personal and sympathetic view of the Gary system during March, 1915. Written for laymen, this series of articles represents popular thinking with specific topic focus in individual articles.

405 Clapp, Elsie Ripley. *Community Schools in Action*.
New York: The Viking Press, 1939, 429 pp.

An intriguing comparative study of experimental
schools in rural locales. The Roger Clark Ballard
Memorial School in Jefferson County, Kentucky, and
the elementary school in Arthurdale, West Virginia.
An early investigation describing community involvement, classroom practices and administrative problems.

406 Clapp, Elsie Ripley. "The Subject Matters in Experimental Education", *Progressive Education*, October-
December, 1926, 370-375.

A very thoughtful analysis of the need to consider
what is being taught in experimental programs. The
writer draws on her experiences at the Junior School
of the famed Rosemary Hall.

407 Clouser, Lucy, Wilma Robinson and Dina Neely. *Educative Experiences Through Activity Units*. Chicago:
Lyons and Carnahan, 1932, 307 pp.

An account of the activities during one year in a
special program in the Kansas City Public Schools.
The development of units, factors related to child
growth and educational goals are clarified through
descriptive material. The philosophy of DeCroly related to the need for activity underlies this experiment in the new education. Reading clubs, circulat-
ing libraries, carpentry are placed into unit structure.

408 Corlett, Albert. "The Dalton Plan in a Senior Boys'
School", *The New Era*, Vol. 18, No. 3, January,
1937, 37-42.

A compact and interesting description of an adap-
tation of the work of Helen Parkhurst. A Dalton Plan
is implemented in an English boys' senior high school
where the conditions necessitate some modifications.
The material is fresh and enlightening.

409 Curry, W. B. *Education in a Changing World*. New
York: W. W. Norton and Company, Inc., 1935,
192 pp.

This volume, written by the headmaster of the
famed Dartington Hall School, is an attempt to place
the new education within the context of the needs of
individuals in rapidly changing societies. The thinking is crisp and insightful, reflecting both experience and foresight. Drawing from his own experiences
to illustrate particular issues the author extends the

work at Dartington Hall (to create a civilized community to engage in social life as part of schooling) to a wide audience.

410 DeLima, Agnes. *A School for the World of Tomorrow.* New York: Lincoln School of Teachers College, Columbia University, 1939, 46 pp.

A presentation booklet describing the Lincoln School of Teachers College, New York City. The program is presented along with the design of the group structure. This was one of the earliest progressive schools using a non-graded, integrated approach to grouping. Photographs are included.

411 DeLima, Agnes. *Democracy's High School.* New York: Teachers College, Columbia University, 1941, 90 pp.

A slender descriptive book on the famed Lincoln School high school of Teachers College. This material is particularly interesting in terms of providing a picture of curriculum and practices at this level. A great deal more has been written on the lower school. This pioneer attempt to introduce progressive methods at the secondary level is sympathetically documented.

412 DeLima, Agnes. *Little Red Schoolhouse.* New York: The Macmillan Company, 1942, 355 pp.

A remarkable accounting of the Little Red Schoolhouse, founded by Elizabeth Irwin in New York City. This pioneering educational experiment was responsible for the future direction of a great deal that occured in public school curriculum revision in New York City. The grade-by-grade curriculum is detailed. Procedures for working with school personnel and parents are included. The school budget appears in the appendix providing interesting material for reflection and placing this innovative operation into fiscal perspective.

413 Dewey, Evelyn. *The Dalton Laboratory Plan.* New York: E. P. Dutton Company, 1922, 173 pp.

A review of the laboratory plan formulated by Helen Parkhurst and implemented in a few schools in England and America. The exposition is clear and helps relate the active dimensions of this plan to those practices originating at the Dewey School. This plan of individualized instruction reflects the influence of Maria Montessori and Helen Parkhurst.

414 Dewey, John. "Introduction to the Work of Group
        III", *The Elementary School Record*, 1900,
        12-21.

        The inter-relatedness of socialization and con-
        cept learning of young children in classrooms is
        treated with specific examples of activities and
        interactions among six year old children at the Labor-
        atory School (founded by Dewey and his wife in 1896).
        An early record of group work practices of interest.

415 Dix, Lester. *A Charter for Progressive Education.*
        New York: Teachers College, Columbia University,
        1939, 107 pp.

        The Lincoln School, New York City, is described
        in great detail in this volume. This is a case study
        approach including: material on the basic principles
        underlying such a school, means of planning curricu-
        lum, resources for curriculum development and imple-
        mentation, scheduling of the program and teacher
        training. The book is both a practical guide and a
        serious contribution to considerations related to
        curriculum and design. The format of the book pro-
        vides for a clear picture of possibilities within
        schools as they related to teacher-child, staff-
        parent relationships. The author was principal of
        the Lincoln School.

416 Gage-Dell, B. Marie and Frances Elwyn. "The Parents
        of Hessian Hills", *Progressive Education*, Vol.
        VIII, No. 8, December, 1930, 408-411.

        This modest article on the role parents played at
        the Hessian Hills School, Croton-on-Hudson, New York,
        provides a model for parent involvement that would
        stand up to current use. The active involvement of
        parents in the progressive movement has been meagrely
        reported in the literature. Photographs are included.

417 Garrison, Charlotte G. *Permanent Play Materials for
        Young Children.* New York: Charles Schibner's
        Sons, 1926, 122 pp.

        This interesting volume, the results of several
        years of experimentation at the Horace Mann School
        in New York City, provides a guide to the selection
        of materials and equipment for early childhood pro-
        grams. The material is of value to practitioners
        today. The forward by Patty S. Hill is particularly
        interesting since she discusses both the earlier
        Froebel materials and the Montessori materials and
        approach in terms of the then current practices at
        the Mann School. Chapters are set up by curriculum

areas and photography of children engaged in activities with the materials and equipment help bring a sense of timeliness to the text. This is an important resource volume.

418 Goodlander, Mabel. *Education Through Experience*. New York: The Bureau of Educational Experiments, Ethical Culture School, 1922, 36 pp.

A report on the four year experiment at the Ethical Culture School, New York City.This venture involved an "experimental class" having one teacher (the author) for a period of three years during which time "newer theories" in education were tried. Programs for each year are described and samples of children's work are included.

419 Hartman, Gertrude. *Finding Wisdom*. New York: The John Day Company, 1938, 147 pp.

An intimate and inspired accounting of a year at the Avery Coonley School at Downer's Grove, Illinois. The school through its founders, Mrs. Coonley and Miss Morse, attempted to bring Dewey's philosophical ideas into educational practice. The physical beauty of the school and the range of activities are shown to advantage in the photographs. Examples of children's work and work with parents are included.

420 Henley, Faye. "An Experiment in the Francis W. Parker School of San Diego, California", *Kindergarten Review*, Vol. XXV, 1914-1915, 492-498.

The western version of the famous Francis W. Parker School in Chicago is described by one of its teachers. The experiment was based on the premise that social motives could be found for most school work and individual initiative could be developed. A description of the activities (individual cases are used for illustrative purposes) and comparison between kindergartners and primary children in this school and others is provided.

421 Horrall, Albion Harris et al. *Let's Go to School: Integrative Experiments in a Public Elementary School*. New York: McGraw-Hill Book Company, 1938, 434 pp.

A beautiful record of progressive practices in action in the San Jose Public Schools. The authors represent both the teaching and administrative staff and the narrative reflects a comprehensive view of school life. Photographs by George Stone are outstanding and bring visual veracity to the text. The material is of more than historical interest.

422   Isaacs, Susan. *The Nursery Years*. London: Routledge
       & Kegan Paul, 1929, 138 pp.

       A guide for parents of both a developmental and
       educational nature. This work appeared after Isaac's
       break with Geoffrey Pyke with whom she collaborated
       on the Malting House School. The material reflects
       the experiences gained at Malting House. The early
       study of the child as a focus for progressive educa-
       tional practices is at the heart of the volume.

423   Johnson, Harriet. *Children in the Nursery School*.
       New York: The John Day Company, 1928, 325 pp.
       Reprinted 1972, Agathon Press, Introduction by
       Barbara Biber.

       The author was the director and founder of The
       Nursery School, an experimental school for toddlers
       (14-36 months old). This is a record of eight years
       which provides material on philosophy, planning and
       operations of the school. Anecdotes, examples of
       children's work, curriculum considerations, record-
       keeping and photos are profusely distributed through-
       out the text. An early work of one of the pioneers
       in the early childhood movement whose activities pro-
       vided a substantive base for educators of young
       children in the progressive era.

424   Johnson, Harriet. *A Nursery School Experiment*.
       New York: The Bureau of Educational Experi-
       ments, 1924, 84 pp.

       This report on the experiment in pre-school edu-
       cation with children under three years of age pro-
       vides material related to the planning, organizing
       and workings of a laboratory situation for the study
       of growth and development. A seminal work on obser-
       vation conditions and practices for children under
       three. The apparatus used in the school with children
       is described in detail. Record-keeping emerges as an
       important dimension of the work within the school.
       Excerpts and photos of records are provided. A chap-
       ter on music in the nursery school was written by
       Maude Stewart and describes in detail the program for
       1923-1924. Responses of the children to the music
       program are recorded as daily anecdotes.

425   Lewis, Mary. *An Adventure with Children*. New York:
       The Macmillan Company, 1928, 250 pp.

       A very personal account by the principal of the
       Park School, Cleveland, Ohio. A record of twelve
       year's working and playing with children within a

school setting. The day-to-day problems of children and adults within such a setting are interestingly revealed. A quiet book about a living and beautiful school filled with flowers, care and love. The aesthetic dimension of life is central to the program offered. DeCroly visited the school and his effect is discussed.

426 Lynch, A. J. *Individual Work and the Dalton Plan.* London: George Philip & Sons, Ltd., 1925, 264 pp.

A description of the experimental work conducted at West Green School, Tottenham, Great Britain, following the Dalton Plan. This comprehensive study carefully documents the operation of a Dalton school. Floor plans, contract design, subject requirements, teacher responsibilities and syllabi, as well as tests for English composition, literature, language, geography, history, arithmetic, drawing, natural sciences are set forth in great detail. A revealing and substantial contribution of a functioning progressive program.

427 Mayhew, Katherine C. and A. C. Edwards. *The Dewey School: The Laboratory School of the University of Chicago, 1896-1903.* New York: D. Appleton-Century, 1936, 489 pp. (Reprinted 1966, New York: Atherton Press)

The development and organization of the Dewey School is set forth with care and regard. The text provides an important documentation of this earliest experiment in progressive education. The relatedness of child growth and curriculum changes emerges through this most readable text.

428 MacConnell, Charles et al. *New Schools for a New Culture.* New York: Harper & Brothers, 1953, (revised edition), 229 pp.

A highly detailed account of the Core Program developed in the Evanston Township High School, Illinois. Originally written in 1943 this updated version includes the acceptance of the program as a department in the school system. The New School was originally (1937) organized in collaboration with Northwestern University, the Core Program was evolved as its formalized and permanent structure in the 1950's. An experiment of interest to those interested in administration and supervision as well as the curriculum of the 1940's and 1950's. An exposition and clarification of schools engaged in preparation for citizenship in a democracy. An appraisal of the value of such a program is made. The role of parents in the

education of the adolescent is covered rather fully
in a chapter, "A Neglected Resource".

429 McMurray, F. M. *A School in Action: Data on Children, Artists and Teachers a Symposium.* New York:
E. P. Dutton & Company, 1922, 344 pp.

The use of artists in the schools is described in
this account of the work of Joanne Bird Shaw at the
Bird School, Peterborough. This unique school is
reflected in a series of papers by an impressive
group: Padraic Colum and John Merrill (literature),
Earnest Block and Elsa Campbell (nusic), Florence
Mateer and Walter Dearborn (testing and psychological
laboratory). Program material is presented; detailed
anecdotal material is included and psychological pro-
files are developed for selected children.

430 Parkhurst, Helen. *Education on the Dalton Plan.*
New York: E. P. Dutton & Company, Inc., 1922,
214 pp.

A personal accounting of the implementation of the
Dalton Plan. The Plan is carefully detailed chapter
by chapter; principles, practices, application, as-
signments, graphing of progress and a full record
of a year's experiment at an English secondary and
elementary school. The appendix provides curriculum
material of more than historical interest. Comments
by administrators and children on the plan reveal
problem areas and attitudes to such change. A valuable resource volume.

431 Peabody, F. G. *Education for Life.* New York:
Doubleday and Company, 1919, 393 pp.

The beginnings of the Hampton Institute are detailed. The use of an active, industrial arts program is described. The philosophy, practices and
personnel involved in this original educational
establishment in the South reveal a sense of community and purpose.

432 Pratt, Caroline. *I Learn From Children.* New York:
Simon and Schuster, 1948, 104 pp.

A very personal view of the City and Country
School, New York City, by one of its founders. A
pioneer in the new education describes practices
by age group and discusses the administrative problems involved in such a school. The child development point of view is strongly supported throughout
the text.

433 Pratt, Caroline (ed.) *Experimental Practices in the City and Country School*. New York: E. P. Dutton & Company, 1924, 302 pp.

A comprehensive look at the methods and philosophy practiced at the City and Country School, New York. The pioneering work in activity-centered curriculum is carefully detailed. Description of age-level curriculum is described.

434 Pratt, Caroline and Jessie Stanton. *Before Books*. New York: Adelphi Company, 1926, 347 pp.

A record of the City and Country School, New York City, by its founder and one of the original teachers. This record of the experimental practices and pioneering efforts is documented through school records in the form of observations and daily notes. The periods covered are: 1920-1921, 1923-1924. The program, the children, staff, buildings, space, furnishings and materials used are described in detail. An important and unique record.

435 Pratt, Caroline and Leila V. Stott. *Adventuring with Twelve Year Olds*. New York: Greenberg Publishers, 1927, 193 pp.

A comprehensive account of the work of twelve year olds over a one year period at the City and Country School, New York. This group engaged in group and individual activities and records were kept by both the children and teachers. Illustrative material is most helpful.

436 Reddie, Cecil. *Abbotsholme*. London: G. Allen, 1900, 640 pp.

A beautifully written accounting by the founder of Abbotsholme of the unusual plan to create a society of young men engaged in the process of schooling. His attempt to fuse theory and practice and the creation of a curriculum that was more practical and concrete is shown to advantage in this work. The school was seen as an educational laboratory for boys from 11-18.

437 Slight, Jeanie P. *Living with Children*. Glasgow: Grant Educational Company, 1933, 115 pp.

A personal account of great warmth and particular interest. An accounting of the work at Fieldon School, Manchester, England, with infant classes. Froebel, Montessori, Dewey emerge as theorists of merit and value in school design and program planning. Presentation of the program, activities with the children, value of play in learning, book learning and skill development of young children in an activity-oriented environment are covered. The project method is stressed. Photographs are included.

438 South Philadelphia High School for Girls. *Educating for Responsibility*. New York: The Macmillan Company, 1926, 310 pp.

An unusual accounting of the implementation of the Dalton Plan in a public high school. The material is fresh and enlightening. An introduction by Lucy Wilson reflects the Montessori influence on both Wilson and Parkhurst.

439 Stott, Leila V. *Adventuring with Twelve Year Olds*. New York: Greenberg Publishers, Inc., 1927, 193 pp.

One year (1926) of work with the twelve year old group at the New York City and Country School is described in great detail by the teacher of the group. Time schedules, curriculum content, anecdotes and examples of children's work are included and make for an unusual view of the school activity program. The setting up of a toy company by the group is particularly well chronicled. An unusual account of one year in a progressive private school with pre-adolescents.

440 Stott, Leila V. *Eight Year Old Merchants*. New York: Greenberg Publishers, Inc., 1928, 158 pp.

A comprehensive view of the work of a group of eight year olds engaged in the central unit of organizing a store. The plans and activities are well described by a classroom teacher committed to this active program in the City and Country School, New York City. This unusual undertaking, the development of a store within the school to manage supplies, was carefully studied and replicated. The relationship of children to the management of the curriculum is detailed. The role of the adults in this setting emerges as that of acute observers and unusual teachers. Anecdotal material is used throughout to provide readers with developmental data on the children as they move through the year.

441 Washburne, Carleton W. *Adjusting the School to the Child*. Yonkers-on-Hudson, New York: World Book Company, 1932, 189 pp.

The sub-title of this volume is "Practical First
Steps". The material is drawn from the Winnetka
Public Schools' experiment in educational research and
the new education. The use of the public school system as an educational laboratory is described in detail. This pioneering effort is dealt with in a
broad manner. Substantive material on the individualized instructional procedures in specific curriculum
areas: arithmetic, reading, spelling, social studies,
etc. appears. The administration of such a program
including schedules, personnel evaluations, etc. is
clarified with the aid of facsimile documents. The
need to relate such change to the community in order
to obtain support is carefully explained.

442 Washburne, Carleton W. "The Inception of the Winnet-
     ka Technique", *American Association of University
     Women Journal*, Vol. 23, April, 1930, 129-134.

     An early view of the beginnings of the Winnetka
Plan by the superintendent of schools. The problems
of implementing such a large scale plan are discussed.

443 Washburne, Carleton W. and Sidney Marland. *Winnetka:
     The History and Significance of an Educational Ex-
     periment*. Englewood Cliffs, N. J.: Prentice-Hall,
     1963, 402 pp.

     Almost fifty years of educational activity are
covered in this volume. The authors, superintendents
of the Winnetka Schools for all but thirteen years
of that period, have each written an account. Part
One provides material on the origin of the experiment,
in individualization of the curriculum by areas, the
nursery school, selection and salaries of teachers,
relations with the community and effects of change.
Part Two presents the contrast, seen as a developmental one, with particular emphasis on the development
of the curriculum along individual lines. This volume helps to clarify the laboratory nature of this
system over a long period of time. An appendix contains facsimiles of goal record cards for all subjects, parent-conference guides and records and the
stanine achievement and ability profile charts (currently modified within many systems). A classic history of this important school system's experiment
with the new education.

444 Winsor, Charlotte (ed.) *Experimental Schools Re-
     visited*. New York: Agathon Press, Inc., 1973,
     335 pp.

     This collaboration represents twelve articles in-
cluded in eight bulletins of the Bureau of Educational

Experiments with an introduction by Charlotte Winsor. The focus is on early childhood and the schools represented include Caroline Pratt's The Play School, Margaret Naumberg's The Children's School and the Teacher's College Playground. Each account is complete. The material represents a central source of reportage on original ideas related to the beginnings of scientific observation of group experiences with young children and the design of facilities for very young children. The pioneers speak for themselves through these early accounts of their work.

445 Wofford, Kate V. *Modern Education in the Small Rural School*. New York: The Macmillan Company, 1938, 582 pp.

Rural schools are examined in terms of the use of newer experimental techniques in such settings. A child-growth and child-study approach is espoused. An interesting volume in terms of the changes toward a more open and relevant curriculum in a rural setting.

446 Zyve, Claire T. *Willingly to School*. New York: Round Table Press, 1934, 108 pp.

A pictorial accounting (photographed by Wendell MacRae) of school life at the Fox Meadow School in Scarsdale, New York. The accompanying text provides a running commentary on school life in a progressive school. Photographs and text are well balanced and offer an interesting view of setting and activities.

Crosslistings:

J ADMINISTRATION

447 Adams, Fay. *The Initiation of an Activity Program into a Public School.* New York: Bureau of Publications, Teachers College, Columbia University, 1934, 80 pp.

The introduction to this study could apply to the current open education movement. The study was undertaken to help clarify the transitional problems of moving a program in small private schools into larger public school settings. A review of previous investigations is included. The study design includes interviews and ratings from almost 1000 educators (student teachers, teachers, administrators, supervisors, college faculty). Problems are stated and possible solutions for resolution offered. A slender and useful book.

448 Burr, Samuel Engle. *An Introduction to Progressive Education (The Activity Plan).* Revised edition. Cincinnati, Ohio: C. A. Gregory Company, 1937, 84 pp.

This is a booklet on the development of progressive education with special attention given to The Activity Plan. The material was prepared for administrators to familiarize them with the movement and help facilitate work with staff in changeover from traditional programs. A clear statement and introduction. Includes bibliography. Material on each of the curriculum areas. Descriptive material on "Unit of Work". The focus on administrative aspects is an interesting one.

449 Burr, Samuel Engle. *A School in Transition.* Boston: The Christopher Publishing House, 1937, 210 pp.

A study of the activity program. The process of change during a three year period in a public school moving from a traditional plan to the activity program. A careful documentation.

450 Callahan, Raymond. *Education and the Cult of Efficiency*. Chicago: University of Chicago Press, 1962, 279 pp.

An examination of the trends beginning in the twenties and thirties which gave rise to the "cost-effective" factor in educational planning. This aspect of the new movement has received little attention in the literature. The material presented is substantial.

451 Clapp, Elsie Ripley. *The Use of Resources in Education*. New York: Harper & Brothers, 1952, 174 pp.

Dewey wrote the introduction to this interesting work. He looks at the past and present and comments on the fixed quality emerging in the progressive context. He points to the future as a time that requires morally and intellectually able adults. The text provided guidelines for the assembly of a wide range of resources that could facilitate planning of sound educational programs.

452 Gustin, Margaret and Margaret Hays. *Activities in the Public School*. Chapel Hill: The University of North Carolina Press, 1934, 290 pp.

A practical guide for educators of the child-centered curriculum based on materials from actual classroom situations in Cartaret and Craven Counties, North Carolina. The authors supervised teachers in public schools in a rural setting. School expenditures were below the national average, yet the educational level was high. An encouragement for those who felt that the progressive movement was reserved for more affluent suburban areas. The material on classroom centers seems very related to current open classroom practices. Case studies of selected children are included, as well as photographs of children and activities.

453 Hill, Clyde M. *Educational Progress and School Administration*. New Haven: Yale University Press, 1936, 400 pp.

A memorial volume prepared by the associates of Frank Ellsworth Spaulding on the occasion of his retirement as Sterling Professor of Educational Administration at Yale. The essays are particularly well written and prepared especially for this volume. They reflect the judicious nature of its editor and range from the pre-school (Arnold Gesell) to research in school administration (Milton Cummings).

454 Meyers, Edna. "Experimental Possibilities in the
     Public Schools", *Progressive Education*, Vol. IX,
     No. 1, January, 1932, 22-28.

     An account of a Chicago principal's involvement
     in the planning and implementation of a progressive
     plan in a public school. The design is most care-
     fully described. The findings of the study indicate
     some of the needed areas for further work. Thought-
     ful rendering of action research on the administra-
     tive school level.

455 Mohl, Raymond. "Schools, Politics, and Riots: The
     Gary Plan in New York City, 1914-1917", *Paeda-
     gogica Historica*, Vol. 15, No. 1, 1975, 39-72.

     A fascinating accounting of the political realities
     surrounding the introduction of the Gary Plan in New
     York City schools. The political and social matrix of
     educational decision making is highly visible in the
     reportage on this experiment in educational change
     within a large school system.

456 Mohl, Raymond. "Urban Education in the Twentieth
     Century: Alice Barrows and the Platoon School
     Plan", *Urban Education*, Vol. 9, No. 3, October,
     1974, 213-238.

     An historical review of the work of Alice Barrows
     in bringing the Platoon System developed by Dr. Wirt
     in Gary, Indiana, into the mainstream of New York City
     education. This piece makes a good companion piece to
     Mohl's "Schools, Politics, and Riots".

457 McCall, William and John Loftus. "America's Largest
     City Experiments with a Crucial Educational Prob-
     lem", *Teachers College Record*, Vol. 38, No. 7,
     April, 1937, 602-606.

     The reporting of the intended experimental use of
     the Activity Program by the Board of Education of
     New York City detailing criteria for inclusion of
     schools and personnel. Administrative planning for
     this program is outlined. Relates to change consid-
     erations in a large urban system.

458 McKown, Harry. *Activities in the Elementary School*.
     New York: McGraw Hill Book Company, Inc., 1938,
     473 pp.

     The role of activities in integrated intra-class
     projects and extra-class school programs. The pro-
     ject approach as utilized through activities. Admin-

istrative problems, supervisory patterns, room organization, assembly programs, drama, music, school publications are discussed from a functional point of
view. Related bibliographic material for each chapter.

459 McKown, Harry. *School Clubs*. New York: The Macmillan Company, 1930, 498 pp.

Manual of school club organization and objectives.
This plan to extend the curriculum offered in high
schools through school clubs that would permit interest grouping of students became a popular one within
the progressive movement. The administration and
supervision of such clubs is carefully detailed. The
clubs are classified into sixteen units and each one
is fully developed in terms of operations. Relates
to both curriculum expansion and the idea of the extended day.

460 Newlon, John. "The Role of Administrative Leadership
in the Reconstruction of Education", *Teachers College Record*, Vol. 36, December, 1934, 213-223.

Director of the Lincoln School details the problems
in educational leadership at the administrative level
by reviewing earlier patterns and examining patterns
of the past forty years (1890-1920). A call for educational statesman is made as a result of the social
role and conflicts pressuring the schools.

461 Oppenheimer, J. *The Visiting Teacher Movement*.
New York: The Public Education Association of
the City of New York, 1924, 203 pp.

A detailed history of the visiting teacher movement. This movement to place teachers within the
home had an important role to play in helping meet
the needs of problem children. Its effect on the cli-
mate of schools is also of interest. In effect, those
children who could not manage the school situation
were provided with teachers on their homes. Administration of such a program is detailed.

462 Public Administration Service. *The Public School
System of Gary, Indiana*. Gary, Indiana: Public
Administration Service, 1955, 195 pp.

A report of a survey conducted by the Public Administration Service for the Board of Trustees of the
School, City of Gary. The one year survey includes
detailed analysis of the major phases of school operation (financing, curriculum, plants, staffing). The
report is of particular value when contrasted with the
findings of the Flexner and Bachman study of 1916 on

the same system. The opportunity to view a single
system over a number of decades is unique.

463 Sanders, Frederic W. *The Reorganization of Our
       Schools*. Boston: The Palmer Company, 1915,
       120 pp.

    The development of postulates related to education-
al change is extended through a clear presentation of
suggestions of a practical nature for the organization of schools. An early call for a vertical reorganization from nursery through high schools. The
author, principal of the Lincoln School, Nebraska
and honorary fellow of Clark University was a disciple
of G. Stanley Hall and John Dewey. The ideas presented are clear, cogent, and surprisingly fresh,
e.g. morning, afternoon and evening classes for adolescents. The detailing of comprehensive change based
on child development principles is an early attempt to
unify study of the child with changes in educational
structures and curriculum.

464 Search, Preston W. *An Ideal School for Looking
       Forward*. New York: D. Appleton, 1901, 357 pp.

    Starting with the premise of the need to recon-
struct our educational system, the author, fellow at
Clark University, superintendent of schools, principal
and teacher, provides details for a new view. G. Stanley Hall, in his preface to this work, indicates that
the argument provided is a starting point for a progressive view of education. School plants, architecture, room settings, courses of study, etc. are crit-
icised and imagined: e.g. an early call for educational parks. An interesting work in retrospect.

465 Stevens, Marion P. *A Classified List of Primary
       Furnishings, Apparatus, and Materials*. New York:
       The Ethical Culture Society, 1930, 32 pp.

    A short but interesting presentation on the mater-
ials needed to implement an activity program built
around social learning and directed goals. The early
childhood program materials and equipment described
will be of interest to those working in open classroom early childhood situations.

466 Youtz, Philip. "School Buildings That Educate",
       Progressive Education, Vol. XIV, No. 3, March,
       1932, 189-194.

    The need for particular attention to building de-
signs for the new education is developed through an
examination of the means and ends of progressive edu-

cation. A critical look at the approach of architects and their interpretation of modern architecture is provacative.

Crosslistings:

    71   Mort
    193   Graymar
    203   Newlon
    342   Kilpatrick
    412   DeLima
    428   MacConnell
    430   Parkhurst
    433-434 Pratt
    441-442 Washburne
    452   Gustin

K PARENT INVOLVEMENT

467 Andrus, Ruth et al. *Discovering Lay Leadership in*
     Parent Education. Albany: The University of
     The State of New York Press, 1935, 108 pp.

     A call for parent involvement in the schools.
     This material was developed to help increase the role
     of lay persons in school management. An important
     part of the progressive plan was the inclusion of
     parents in the school life of children.

468 Andrus, Ruth and May E. Peabody. *The Mental Health*
     of Parenthood. Albany: Child Development and
     Parent Education Bureau, 1934, 42 pp.

     An outline for group discussion utilization with
     parents developed through the New York State Bureau
     of Child Development and Parent Education. This
     bureau worked diligently to bring parents into the
     educational mainstream.

469 Baldwin, Sara and Ernst Osborne. *Home-School Rela-*
     tions: Philosophy and Practice. New York:
     Progressive Education Association, 1935, 142 pp.

     An intensive study of home-school relations under-
     taken through the auspices of the National Council of
     Parent Education, the Progressive Education Associa-
     tion and the Child Development Institute of Teachers
     College, Columbia University. Six schools reflecting
     a broad range (rural, suburban, private, public) par-
     ticipated in the study as field sites. Three major
     areas are covered: the underlying philosophy of
     home-school relations in a variety of schools, how
     the school provides for such relations, and an eval-
     uation of teachers' and parents' interactions and the
     success of such relationships. The material is hand-
     led in two parts, the first is descriptive, the sec-
     ond analytic and suggestive. A short bibliography of
     journal articles is included.

470 Fisher, Dorothy Canfield. *A Montessori Mother*.
     New York: Holt, Rinehart and Winston, Inc.,

1912, 240 pp.

An attempt to bring the author's enthusiasm for
early childhood training with parents to the public.
This work was an important one in its time since it
helped to create an interest in the developmental
needs of the young child and to provide parents with
a basis for aiding in the education of the child
within the home. An intimate book reflecting the
interest and enthusiasm of an unusual woman.

471   Hambridge, Gove. *New Aims in Education*. New York:
      McGraw-Hill Company, 1940, 226 pp.

A book written by a parent involved in the new
education for the lay audience. This interesting
volume is directed to those who needed assurance
about the changes taking place in schools. An interesting contribution in terms of a call for parent involvement.

472   Hill, Gladwin. *A Father Looks at Progressive Educa-
      tion*. Washington. D. C.: National School Pub-
      lic Relations Association, 1954, 16 pp.

The author, chief of the New York Times Bureau in
Los Angeles, describes his enthusiasm for the University Elementary School at the University of California in Los Angeles. Written for the layman,
this first appeared as an article in the ATLANTIC.
It is a narrative built around responses to commonly
expressed questions and criticism of the progressive
movement.

473   Patri, Angelo. *Child Training*. New York: D.
      Appleton & Company, 1922, 434 pp.

A manual for parents dealing with newer practices
in child rearing reflecting progressive thinking.
Material on education in the home and the parents'
role in the child's school life. Patri, an educator,
became a columnist having a regular parent education
syndicated column.

474   Pulliam, Roscoe. *Extra-Instructional Activities of
      the Teacher*. New York: Doubleday-Doran, 1930,
      459 pp.

Problems of discipline, health, attendance, parental relations, etc. considered extra-instructional
are presented within a framework that provides for
positive activities on the part of the classroom
teacher in the newer schools (progressive). An interesting insight into the thrust toward community

and home relations on the part of the schools.

475   Reisner, Elizabeth. "An Activity Program for Parents
        in Parent Education", *Teachers College Record*,
        Vol. 37, April, 1935, 559-565.

        The responsibility of parents related to the home
        life of children is clarified through a presentation
        of work at the Lincoln School and the Horace Mann
        School in New York City with parents. The relation-
        ship of parent and teacher responsibility to the well-
        being of the child is described.

476   Smith, Eugene Randolph. *Education Moves Ahead: A
        Survey of Progressive Methods*. Boston: The
        Atlantic Monthly Press, 1924, 122 pp.

        A series of informal and provocative talks to
        parents and teachers related to the new educational
        methods and a rapidly changing world order. A pro-
        phetic work calling for a collaboration between
        parents and teachers in the physical and moral educa-
        tion of children. A very personal statement that re-
        veals the possibilities of reciprocity between home
        and school.

477   Woodring, Paul. *Let's Talk Sense About Our Schools*.
        New York: McGraw Hill Company, Inc., 1953, 215 pp.

        Parents as consumers of education are the intended
        audience for this book. The role of parents as de-
        cision makers vis-a-vis public education is described.
        The author positions parents in relation to the "new
        education" and the controversies surrounding such
        change are set into an active framework. He insists
        that the public has a responsibility to be well in-
        formed and should take active parts in the direction
        of all aspects of public education. An early view of
        community control by a conservative.

Crosslistings:

         95   Cobb
        105   Dewey
        136   Neill
        405   Clapp
        416   Gage-Dell
        428   MacConnell

L JOURNALS

478 *Bulletins of the Bureau of Educational Experiments.*
     Vols. 1 - 12, 1917-1922. New York: Bureau of
     Educational Experiments, 1917.

     Topical bulletins for the Bureau of Educational
Experiments covering research findings and original
contributions. First publication was on PLAYTHINGS;
the publications reflect an early childhood focus.
Bank Street School of Education houses a complete
file of this early material.

479 *Childhood Education.* Vol. I - , September, 1924 - .
     Baltimore: Williams & Wilkins Company, 1925.

     A monthly (during the academic year) journal de-
voted to current educational practices and ideas.
Volumes I - VI (October, 1924 - June, 1930) appeared
as the official journal of the International Kindergarten Union. Volumes VII - XXIV (October, 1930 -
December, 1948) were the official journal of the
newly named Association for Childhood Education (ACE).
The organization was reconstituted into the Association for Childhood Education International (ACEI) in
January, 1949. Issues appearing during the late
twenties and throughout the thirties reflect the progressive influence at both the early childhood and
primary levels.

480 *Education.* Vol. I - , 1880-1881 - . Boston: New
     England Publishing Company, 1881.

     A bi-monthly international magazine devoted to
science, art, philosophy and literature of education.
This journal was edited by Frank H. Palmer. The
material includes both practical and philosophical
ideas.

481 *Education Digest.* Vol. I - , November, 1935 - .
     Ann Arbor, Michigan, 1935.

     Articles were selected from a variety of journals
for inclusion in this digest.

482 *The Educational Forum.* Vol. I - , November, 1936 - .
     Menasha, Wisconsin: The Executive Council of
     Kappa Delta Pi, 1936.

     The official journal of Kappa Delta Pi appearing
as a monthly during the school year. Book reviews
and current periodical reviews as well as articles
during the thirties reflect progressive trends. Alfred Hall-Quest was its first editor.

483 *Educational Review.* Vol. 1 - 76, January, 1891 -
     October, 1928. New York: Henry Holt and Company,
     1891 - 1928.

     A prominent monthly covering important educational
ideas and practices. Nicholas Murray Butler was editor from 1920 to 1924 and William McAndrew served
as editor from 1924 to 1928. In 1928 the journal
was merged with SCHOOL AND SOCIETY.

484 *Educational Trends.* Vol. 1 - 8, January, 1932 - 1940.
     Evanston, Illinois: School of Education, North-
     western University, 1932.

     A quarterly review providing interpretations of
current research related to classroom instruction and
practices. Research related to educational psychology is included. Initial editors were G. H. Betts,
Paul Witty and E. V. Melby.

485 *The Elementary School Journal.* Vol. 1 - , July,
     1900 - . Chicago: The University of Chicago
     Press, 1900.

     Originally titled THE COURSE OF STUDY, a monthly
publication for teachers and parents sponsored by
the Chicago Institute (Academic and Pedagogic) from
July, 1900 - June, 1901. Starting in July, 1901,
and continuing through July, 1902, it was renamed
THE ELEMENTARY SCHOOL TEACHER AND COURSE OF STUDY;
F. W. Parker was the editor during this period. In
October, 1902, it became THE ELEMENTARY SCHOOL TEACH-
ER and continued with such a title through June, 1914.
The following September it became the ELEMENTARY
SCHOOL JOURNAL. An important periodical throughout
the progressive era.

486 *Elementary School Record.* Vol. I (No. 1 - 9),
     February - December, 1900. Chicago: The Univer-
     sity of Chicago Press, 1900.

     A monthly which developed into a single series of
nine monographs. Originally intended as an educational journal it appeared as one volume in nine

monthly (during the school year) monographs. John
Dewey was its editor.

487 *Frontiers of Democracy.* Vol. 1 - 10, 1934 - 1943.
Washington, D. C.: Progressive Education Association, 1934.

An important journal during the peak years of
the progressive movement. The original title for
the journal was THE SOCIAL FRONTIER (Vol. 1 - 5,
1934 - 1939) which was changed in 1939 (Vol. 6).
The journal reflected a critical attitude toward
education in general and espoused the progressive
trends. George Counts was editor from 1934 - 1937,
followed by G. Hartman, 1937 - 1939. William Kilpatrick was editor from 1939 - 1943.

488 *Harvard Teachers Record.* Vol. I - VI, February,
1931 - 1936. Cambridge: The Harvard Graduate
School of Education, 1931.

This series of six volumes, edited by Charles
Swain Thomas, appeared in quarterly editions under
the auspices of the Harvard Graduate School of Education, the Alumni Association of the School and
the Harvard Teachers Association. Beginning with
Volume VII the title was changed to the HARVARD
EDUCATIONAL REVIEW (1937); current volume 47, 1977.
This journal includes a range of current topic articles and reviews. While the focus tended to weigh
in favor of secondary-level changes during the progressive era, coverage of material is extensive for
primary and college level.

489 *The High School Journal.* Vol. 0, December, 1917,
Vol 1 - , January, 1918 - . Chapel Hill, N. C.:
School of Education, University of North Caro-
lina.

An influential journal published eight times a
year. The original editor was N. W. Walker. Administrative and curriculum matters played a sizable
role in the articles. Current volume 56, 1977.

490 *The High School Quarterly.* Vol. 1 - 25, October,
1912 - June, 1937. Athens, Georgia: University
of Georgia, 1912.

The official journal of the Southern Commission
on Accredited Schools of the Georgia High Schools
and National High Schools Inspectors Association.
This journal was prominent during the early years
of the movement and the reportage included national
issues and practices.

491 *Journal of Educational Method*, a journal of progressive public schools. Vol. 1 - 22, September, 1921 - May, 1943. Washington, D. C.: The Department of Supervisors and Directors of Instruction of the NEA of U.S., 1921.

The official organ of the National Conference on Educational Method, "an association devoted to the improvement of teaching and supervision". James F. Hosic was editor from 1921 to 1939. Lou La Brant filled this position from 1939 through 1943. The journal reflected the impact of the progressive movement in the public sector.

492 *Journal of Educational Psychology*. Vol. 1 - , 1910 - . Baltimore: Warwick and York, Inc., 1910.

A monthly journal during the academic year devoted to experimental psychology, child psychology, educational statistics and hygiene. This journal enjoyed an important place in the academic community during the formative years of progressivism. Its editorial board included: W. C. Bagley, Guy M. Whipple and J. Carleton Bell.

493 *Journal of Experimental Education*. Vol. I - , September, 1932 - . Ann Arbor, Michigan: University of Michigan, 1932.

A technical journal devoted to reporting of research related to newer approaches in education. The first editor was A. S. Barr.

494 *National Education Association Index to Addresses and Proceedings*, 1857 - 1906. Winona, Minn.: 1907, 211 pp.

An index to authors, titles and subjects in the publications of the NEA for the first fifty years of leading articles; compiled by Martha F. Nelson.

495 *National Elementary Principal*. Vol. 1 - , May, 1921 - . Washington, D. C.: Department of Elementary School Principals, National Association of the United States, 1921.

An influential journal during the twenties and thirties reflecting the interests of administrators toward the newer progressive ideas.

496 *National Society for the Study of Education Yearbooks*, 1st, 1895 - . Chicago, 1895.

Approved under the original title of HERBART SOCI-
ETY FOR SCIENTIFIC STUDY OF TEACHING prior to 1901.
The Society changed its name to NATIONAL SOCIETY FOR
THE SCIENTIFIC STUDY OF EDUCATION in 1901 and began
a new series of yearbooks beginning with the number
1. In 1909 the name was again changed to the current
form. However, the numbers of the yearbooks continued. Prominent editors were: Charles A. McMurray
Manfred Holmes, J. Stanley Brown, S. Chester Parker
and Guy M Whipple. Each yearbook is based on a theme
and carried a great deal of weight in the academic
and educational communities.

497 *The Nations Schools.* Vol. I - , January, 1928 - .
Chicago: The Nations Schools Publishing Company,
1928.

An influential journal devoted to administration
of schools. The areas of particular interest were
the equipping, building and administration of schools
at every level. Research findings were the basis for
much that was written during the twenties. The progressive period is given an interesting perspective
through this publication.

498 *New Era.* Vol. 1 - , 1920 - . London: New Education
Fellowship, 1920.

An international review of the new education directed toward both the home and the school. The
articles reflected the interests of the core British
group involved in the more progressive changes occur-
ring in England and the Continent. The first editors
were Beatrice Ensor and A. S. Neill.

499 *New Republic.* Vol. 1 - , November, 1917 - . New
York: The Republic Publishing Company, 1917.

A weekly review of opinion including educational
matters of interest to the layman. During the twenties and thirties individual issues ran articles in
a series and as parts of special issues on the newer
educational trends. The journal reflected a liberal
position. An interesting series by Walter Lippman on
testing (1922) was answered by Lewis Terman. Issues
on individual progressive schools appeared in 1924.
A special series on the state of progressive education appeared in 1930.

500 *Pedagogical Seminary.* Vol. I - , January, 1891.
Worcester, Mass.: J. H. Orpha, 1891.

This journal, founded and edited by G. Stanley
Hall, was planned as "an international record of

Educational Literature, Institutions and Progress".
The articles were directed to those interested in
the child-study approach to the development of educational possibilities. It was combined with the JOUR-
NAL OF GENETIC PSYCHOLOGY (Vol. 34, 1927) and was renamed PEDAGOGICAL SEMINARY AND THE JOURNAL OF GENETIC
PSYCHOLOGY. In 1954 (Vol. 55) the name was changed
to the JOURNAL OF GENETIC PSYCHOLOGY.

501   *Progressive Education*. Vol. 1 - 34, April, 1924 -
      July, 1957. Washington, D. C.: The Progressive
      Education Association, 1924.

      The official journal of the Progressive Education
Association. This quarterly review enjoyed a wide
reputation and commanded an important place in the
educational field as the voice of the Association.
The first editor was Gertrude Hartman.

502   *Review of Educational Research*. Vol. 1 - , January,
      1931 - . Washington, D. C.: American Educational
      Research Association, a Department of the National
      Association of the United States, 1931.

      A thematic review enjoying wide currency among
progressive educators and others. The first editor
was F. N. Freeman.

503   *School and Society*. Vol. 1 - 100, January, 1915 -
      May, 1972. New York: Society for the Advance-
      ment of Education, 1915.

      An important journal giving shape to the progres-
sive era. Its first editor was J. McKeen Cattell.
Its frequency varied until 1928 when it combined
with the EDUCATIONAL REVIEW and began to appear as
a monthly. It was later (1930) combined with the
EDUCATION REVIEW.

504   *School Life*. Vol. 1 - 47, August, 1918 - November,
      1964. Washington, D. C.: U. S. Office of Educa-
      tion, 1918.

      A semi-monthly publication of the U. S. Office of
Education ultimately superceded by AMERICAN EDUCATION.
This publication was suspended during the World War
II years (1942-1945). It served a wide base and
reflected the progressive trends and practices of
the time.

505   *The School Review*. Vol. 1 - , January, 1893 - .
      Chicago: The University of Chicago Press, 1893.

A monthly devoted to secondary education. Prior
to the twenties, this journal was a leading organ
for the more progressive ideas in scientific education and management of the high school.

506   *The Social Frontier.* Vol. 1 - 5, 1934 - 1939. Wash-
        ington, D. C.: Progressive Education Association,
        1934.

        See FRONTIERS OF DEMOCRACY.

507   State Journals.
        Alabama School Journal
        Arizona Teacher
        Baltimore Bulletin of Education
        California Teacher
        California Teachers Association - Journal
        Chicago School Journal
        Colorado School Journal
        The Connecticut Teacher
        Florida Educator Association Journal
        Florida School Bulletin
        Georgia Education Journal
        Idaho Journal of Education
        The Illinois Teacher
        Indiana Teacher
        Journal of Arkansas Education
        Kansas Teacher
        Kentucky School Journal
        Louisiana Teachers Association
        Louisiana Schools
        Maine Schools
        Massachusetts Teacher
        Michigan Education Journal
        Minnesota Journal of Education
        Montana Education
        Nebrasks Education Journal
        New Jersey Education Review
        New Mexico School Review
        New York Education (NYU)
        New York State Education
        New York Teachers Monographs (Teachers Monographs)
        The North Central Association Quarterly
        Ohio Education Monthly
        Ohio Schools
        Oklahoma Teacher
        Peabody Journal of Education
        Pennsylvania School Journal
        Pennsylvania State Education Association
        Pittsburgh Schools
        South Carolina Educator
        South Dakota Education Association Journal
        The Tennessee Teacher
        Texas Outlook

Utah Education Review
The Virginia Teacher (Virginia Journal of Education)
Washington Education Journal
The West Virginia School Journal of Education
Wisconsin Journal of Education
Wyoming Education News

State journals played a large part in administrative practices and revealed local needs and activities. Some of these journals achieved wider circulation as a result of the content. The progressive era is reflected in many of the articles.

508   *Studies in Education.* Vol. I - II, 1896 - 1897.
       California: Stanford University, 1896.

A volume series devoted to child study. This material, edited by Earl Barnes, reflected the interest in the developmental needs of the child as a focus for educational planning which was to become so important in the next quarter century.

509   *Teachers College Record.* Vol. 1 - , January, 1900 - .
       New York: The Columbia University Press, 1900.

A journal "devoted to the Practical Problems of Elementary and Secondary Education and the Professional Training of Teachers". Its first editor was James E. Russell. This journal was supported by Teachers College and had as its purpose to provide both faculty and students of the college with a wide view of practices within schools. It was also intended to be used as an in-service professional journal for graduates. The journal enjoyed wide circulation during the twenties and thirties and wielded a great deal of influence in both professional and public sectors.

AUTHOR INDEX

Entry numbers, rather than page numbers, are used to locate items.

Burton, William H. (230, 330)
Butts, R. Freeman and Lawrence A. Cremin (14)

Callahan, Raymond (450)
Carey, Alice et al. (231)
Caswell, Hollis and Dook S. Campbell (232)
Cavallo, Dom (233)
Chamberlin, Charles Dean et al. (365)
Chambliss, J. J. (57)
CHILDHOOD EDUCATION (234)
Childs, John L. (58, 59, 60, 93)
Clapp, Elsie Ripley (405, 406, 451)
Clarke, Eric (235)
Class of 1938, University High School (366)
Clouser, Lucy et al. (236, 407)
Cobb, Ernest (186)
Cobb, Stanwood (94, 95)
Cohen, Ronald D. (367)
Cole, Percival R. (96)
Collings, Ellsworth (237, 238, 368)
Cook, H. Caldwell (239)
Corlett, Albert (408)
Counts, George S. (97, 187, 188)
Cowell, C. C. (369)
Cox, P. W. L. (240)
Crawford, C. C. and L. P. McDonald (331)
Cremin, Lawrence A. (15, 61)
Crow, Charles (241)
Cubberly, Ellwood P. (98)
Culverwell, E. P. (242)
Curry, W. B. (409)
Curti, Merle (62)
Curtis, Nell C. (243)
Cusden, Phoebe (153)

Dalcroze, Emile Jacques (244)
Darroch, Alexander (63)

DeLima, Agnes (410, 411, 412)
Dell, Floyd (99)
Demashkevich, Michael (189)
DePancier, Ida (16)
Dewey, Alice C. (245)
Dewey, Evelyn (413)
Dewey, John (64, 65, 66, 67, 100, 101, 102, 103, 104, 105, 190, 191, 246, 247, 248, 249, 250, 251, 414)
Dill, Nancy (252)
Dix, Lester (415)
Dottrens, Robert (154)
Dropkin, Ruth and Arthur Obier (eds.) (17)
Drost, Walter H. (18)
Dworkin, Martin S. (106)

Eakright, Jessie and Bess Young (253)
Elementary Curriculum Series, Territory of Hawaii (254)
Elementary Teachers and Supervisors of the State of Utah (255)
Everett, Samuel (107)

Featherstone, W. B. (256)
Fediaevsky, Vera and Patty Smith Hill (155)
Feinberg, Walter (108)
Ferriere, Adolphe (157)
Fisher, Dorothy Canfield (470)
Flexner, Abraham (192, 370)
Forest, Ilse (257, 332, 371)
Fowler, B. P. (258)
The Francis W. Parker School (259)
Froebel, Friederich (68)

Gage-Dell, B. Marie and Frances Elwyn (416)
Garrison, Charlotte G. (417)
Gates, Arthur (372, 373)
Gerwig, George W. (109)
Gesell, Arnold (110, 111)
Giles, Harry H. (112)
Good, H. G. (19)
Goodenow, Ronald (20)
Goodlander, Mabel (418)

Graham, Patricia Albjerg
  (21)
Grant, Cecil (158)
Gray, William (333)
Graymar, Thurra (193)
Greene, Katherine (374)
Greene, Maxine (22)
Gunther, Theresa C. (375)
Gustin, Margaret and
  Margaret Hays (452)

Hall, Mary Ross (376)
Hamaide, Amelie (113)
Hambridge, Gove (471)
Harmer, Althea (260)
Hart, Joseph Kimmont (114)
Hartman, Gertrude (261,
  262, 419)
Heaton, K. L. et al. (334)
Heffron, Ida C. (335)
Henley, Faye (420)
Herbart, Johann F. (115,
  116)
Hildreth, Gertrude (263)
Hill, Clyde M. (453)
Hill, Gladwyn (472)
Hill, Patty (ed.) (264)
Hissong, Clyde (117)
Hollingshead, Arthur D.
  (265)
Hollins, T. B. (194)
Holmes, Larry E. (159)
Hook, Sidney (195)
Hopkins, L. T. and James
  Mendelhall (377)
Horne, Herman H. (69)
Horowitz, Helen (23)
Horrall, Albion Harris et
  al. (421)
Hosic, James and Sara
  Chase (266)
Hughes, Avah Willyn (267)
Hulbard, David (24)
Hymes, James L. Jr. (25)

Institution: The Child-
  ren's Friends (159)
Irwin, Elizabeth and
  Louis A. Marks (268)
Isaacs, Susan (118, 119,
  422)

James, William (336)
Johnson, Harriet (423, 424)
Johnson, Marietta (269)
Jones, Thomas Jesse (270)
Judd, Charles (70, 337)

Kandel, I. L. (160, 161, 196,
  197, 338, 378)
Kavier, Clarence J. (26, 198)
Keliher, Alice V. (339)
Kelley, Earl C. (120, 340)
Keohane, Mary (162)
Kilpatrick, William Heard
  (121, 122, 123, 124, 199,
  200, 274, 341, 342)
Kirkpatrick, E. A. (125)
Klapper, Paul (275)
Krackowizer, Alice M. (276)

LaBrant, Lou (27)
Lambert, Clara (343)
Lane, Robert H. (126, 277,
  344)
Langford, Howard (127)
Lawson, M. D. and R. C.
  Peterson (28)
Lay, Wilhelm August (128)
Lee, Joseph (278)
Lewis, Mary (425)
Lilge, Frederic (29)
Loftus, John (379)
Lord Allen of Hurtwood
  (ed.) (30)
Lynch, A. J. (426)

Maguire, Edward R. (279)
Makarenko, A. (164)
Mallon, Paul R. (201)
Maritain, Jacques (129)
Marot, Mary (380)
Marraro, Howard (165)
Mayhew, Katherine and
  A. C. Edwards (427)
Mearns, Hughes (280, 281)
Meiklejohn, Alexander
  (31)
Melvin, A. Gordon (282,
  345, 346)

Robbins, C. I. (141)
Robinson, Virginia P.
   (386)
Roman, Frederick W.
   (168)
Ross, Dorothy G. (40)
Rousseau, Jean J. (75)
Rugg, Harold (41, 142,
   206, 305, 355)
Rusk, Robert (387)
Russell, Bertrand (76)
Ryan, W. Carson (388)

Salisbury, Ethel (306)
Salz, Arthur and Smith,
   Mortimer (207)
Sanders, Frederic W.
   (463)
Sandifer, Sister M. R.
   (208)
Sargent, Porter (209)
Saucier, W. A. (77)
Schoenchen, Gustav G.
   (143)
Search, Preston (464)
Sizer, Nancy F. (169)
Skidelsky, Robert (42)
Slavson, S. R. (307)
Slight, Jeanie P. (437)
Sloman, Laura Gillmore
   (356)
Smith, Eugene Randolph
   (357, 389, 476)
Smith, E. Sharwood (43)
Smith, Mortimer (210,
   211, 212)
Smith, Nila Blanton
   (308, 358)
Snell, Reginald (170)
Spears, Harold (309)
Specht, Minna and A.
   Rosenberg (171)
Stevens, Marion P.
   (310, 465)
Stevenson, John A.
   (145)
Stewart, William A. C.
   (172)
Stiles, Dan (pseudo.)
   (311)
South Philadelphia High
   School for Girls (438)

Stolper, J. R. and H. O. Penn
   (312)
Stoddard, George and Beth G.
   Wellman (313)
Storm, Grace (314)
Stormzand, Martin (390)
Stott, Leila V. (439, 440)
Strickland, Ruth G. (359)
Stuerm, Francis (173)
Stull, DeForest (315)

Thayer, V. T. et al. (316)
Thomas, Milton and Herbert
   Schneider (44)
Thomas, William and Dorothy
   Swaine (317)
Thorndike, E. L. (145)
Thorndike, Robert et al.
   (391)
Tippett, James (318, 319)
Tyler, Ralph W. (ed.)
   (392)

Valentine, P. F. (ed.)
   (45)
van der Eyken, Willem and
   Barry Turner (46)

Waddell, C. W. (320)
Wales, John N. (213)
Ward, Florence (321)
Ware, Caroline (47)
Washburne, Carleton W.
   (78, 146, 147, 174, 393
   441, 442, 443)
Weaver, Anthony (48)
Weber, Julia (49)
Wells, H. G. (50)
Wells, Margaret (322)
Wesley, E. B. (51)
Whipple, Guy M. (52, 323,
   324)
White, Jessie (175)
Wilson, Frank and Agnes
   Burke (394)
Wilson H. and G. M. Wilson
   (148)
Winsor, Charlotte (444)